WHAT'S THE BIG IDEA?

A ground-breaking series for young people which focuses on the hottest issues and ideas around.

Alien Life*
Animal Rights
The Environment
Food*
Genetics
The Media*
The Mind
Nuclear Power
The Paranormal*
Religion
Virtual Reality
Women's Rights

*coming soon

If you would like to make any comments on this book or suggestions for future titles, please write to us at:

What's the Big Idea?
Hodder Children's Books
338 Euston Road
London NW1 3BH

Text copyright © Mary and John Gribbin 1997

Illustrations copyright © Nick Dewar 1997

The right of Mary and John Gribbin and Nick Dewar to be identified as the author and illustrator of the Work has been asserted by them in accordance with the Copyright, Designs and Patents Act 1988.

Cover photograph courtesy of Images Colour Library

Layout by Joy Mutter

Published by Hodder Children's Books 1997

10 9 8 7 6 5 4

ISBN 0 340 65590 9

A Catalogue record for this book is available from the British Library.

Printed and bound in Great Britain by
The Guernsey Press Co. Ltd., Guernsey, Channel Islands

Hodder Children's Books
A division of Hodder Headline plc
338 Euston Road
London NW1 3BH

WHAT'S THE BIG IDEA?

Time and the Universe

by
Mary and John Gribbin

Illustrated by Nick Dewar

Hodder
Children's
Books

a division of Hodder Headline plc

To Jason Lee and Annie Cusworth, our
favourite godchildren.

MG and JG

Contents

Everyone knows what the
time is.

But what is TIME?

Could you explain it to
someone else?

EASON OF THE BIG RAINS

12.0
mid
night

NIGHT

NOR
POL

2.0am

4.0am

6.0a

MAY

APR

MAR

it's... –

what
is
time?

It's not easy, is it? But that's what this book is about.

It will take you on an amazing journey to find out the meaning of time. In the process, you'll travel to the ends of the universe and make some mindboggling discoveries.

Time to begin...

What is time?

The most important thing about time is that THINGS WEAR OUT.

This is called the **Second Law of Thermodynamics.** It is the most important law in the Universe.

that's me! and look what I can do!

SECOND LAW OF THERMO DYNAMICS

NEW
1.

2 WEEKS
2.

3.

strong smell of cheese

1 MONTH.

WHY CAN'T I STOP MY THINGS WEARING OUT?

BECAUSE I'M SO POWERFUL!

The amount of mess in the Universe always increases. A number called **Entropy** measures how messy the Universe is. Entropy always gets bigger.

Tidy your room.

THE ENTROPY MONSTER ↓

1. Oh oh.

↑ tiny and unhappy entropy monster

2. Tidy room...

3. ...but not for long.

I ♥ MESS

4. As the room gets messier, Entropy grows.

So how do rooms get tidied up again? It doesn't happen by magic. Somebody has to work at it!

When someone tidies up and makes a messy room look neat, it looks as if the Second Law of Thermodynamics has been broken. Tidying up has made Entropy smaller in the room.

But outside in the Universe, energy has been used up to make the room tidy.

Work uses up energy, and using up energy always makes Entropy increase!

Everything we do uses up energy from the Universe.

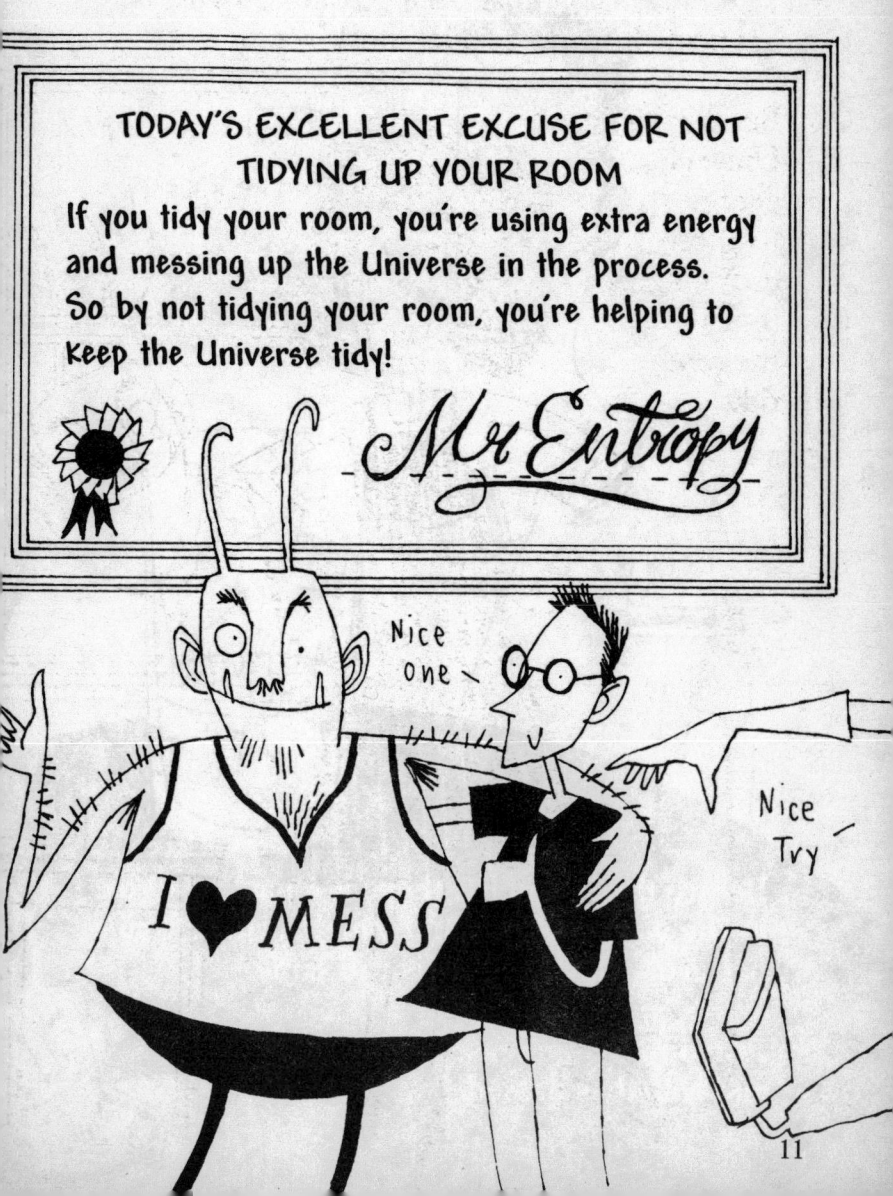

TODAY'S EXCELLENT EXCUSE FOR NOT TIDYING UP YOUR ROOM

If you tidy your room, you're using extra energy and messing up the Universe in the process.
So by not tidying your room, you're helping to keep the Universe tidy!

Mr Entropy

Nice one ~

Nice Try

I ♥ MESS

If Entropy did not increase, there would be no difference between the past and the future.

You can see Entropy increasing and time passing just by popping ice cubes into warm water.

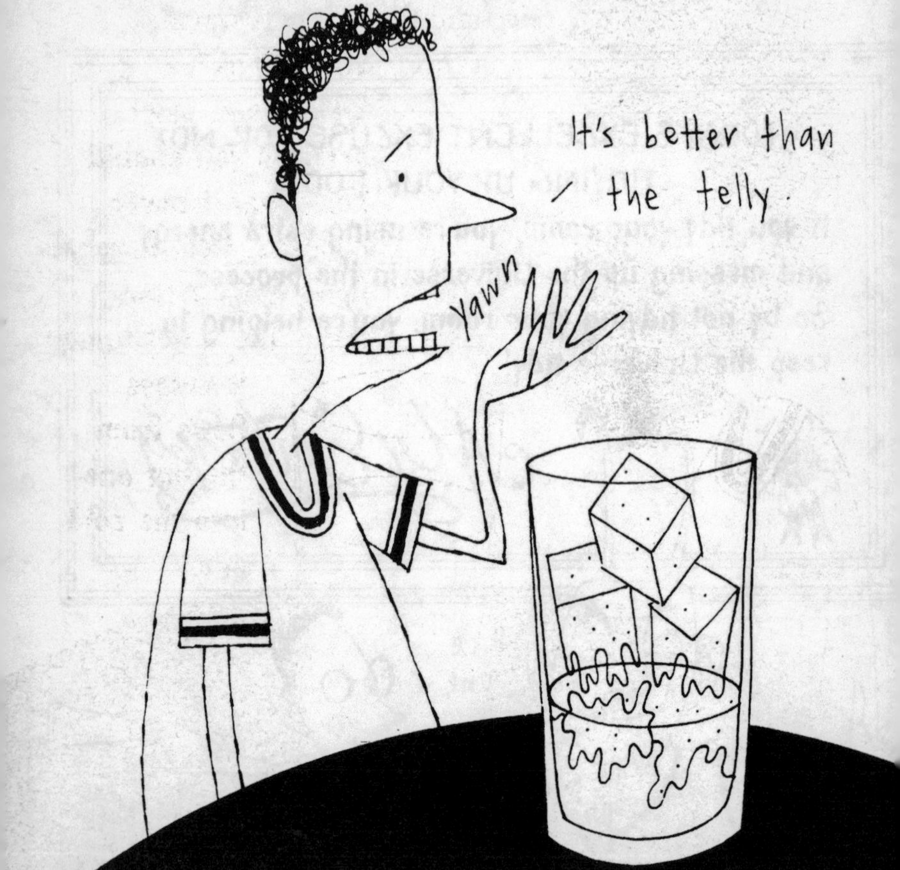

It's better than the telly.

Yawn

Before the ice melts, there is a pattern of ice in the water. After the ice melts, there is no pattern. All the water is the same.

Entropy has increased and time has passed.

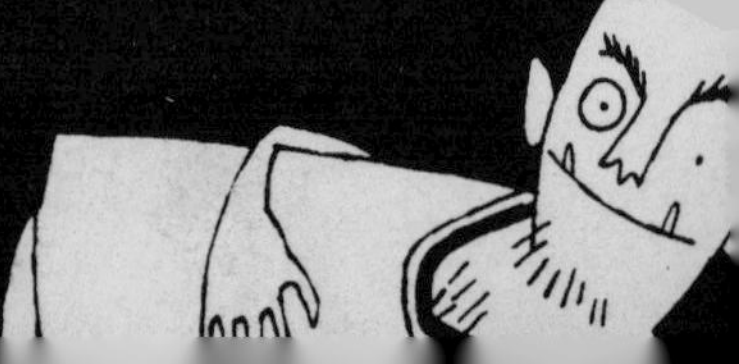

Of course if you are feeling *really* bored you could always try to make time run backwards.

Get a glass of cold water and watch it until some of the water turns into ice and the rest gets warm.

any moment now.

WARNING
Before you start perhaps you should know that it never happens. Heat never flows from a cold thing into a hot thing. It always flows from the hot one into the cold one...

Unless you use energy to make things cold. It's cold inside a fridge because power is being used to pump heat out. So Entropy is increasing somewhere else.

There is another way to understand time.

All of the energy used on
Earth comes from the Sun.*

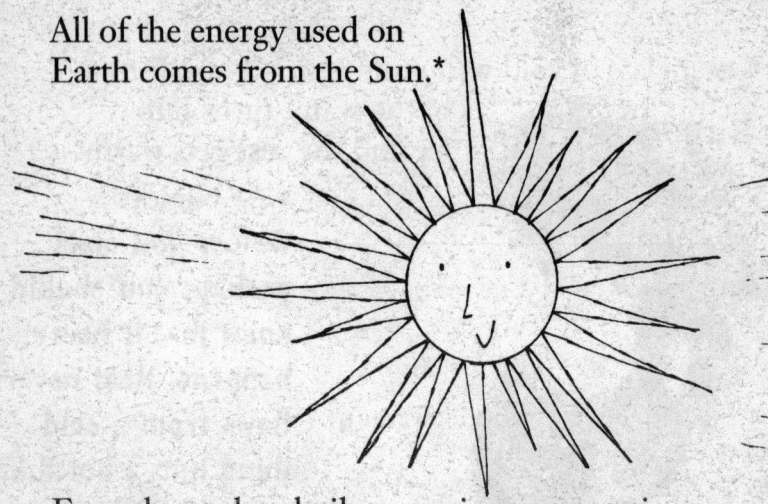

Even the coal and oil we use in power stations
were made by plants that needed sunlight to help
them grow.

plants grow using
energy from the
sun.

they die and rot

and are compressed
to form peat

which in turn becomes
brown coal

It takes a huge amount of energy
to make even simple things,
like glass.

* except for a tiny amount created
by atomic fission.

and finally black coal.

14

You could make time stand still just by taking away the Sun and the stars.

If you got rid of the Sun and the stars, there would be no energy for living things to draw on anywhere in the Universe.

There would be no way to make order out of disorder.

The temperature everywhere would be the same.

Time would not flow.

Nothing at all would happen anywhere.

If everything really could always stay the same, there would be no time at all. It just wouldn't exist.

It is because things wear out that time passes. The everlasting flow of time is like an endless river that carries everything and everyone along with it.

But this doesn't stop there being a past and a future. Time always moves forwards, so you have to make something before it can exist for you to break!

If someone has made a glass in the past 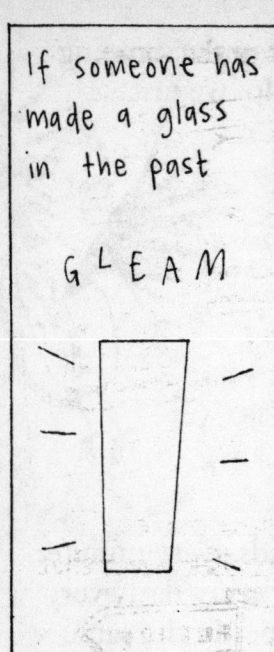	It can be used in the present 	and broken in the future. 

The arrow of time points from the past to the future. But that doesn't explain why we seem to be moving steadily from one to the other. Nobody knows why time flows along like a river instead of being like a set of still photographs.

The most important thing about understanding time is that, no matter what we do, we just can't stop it passing.

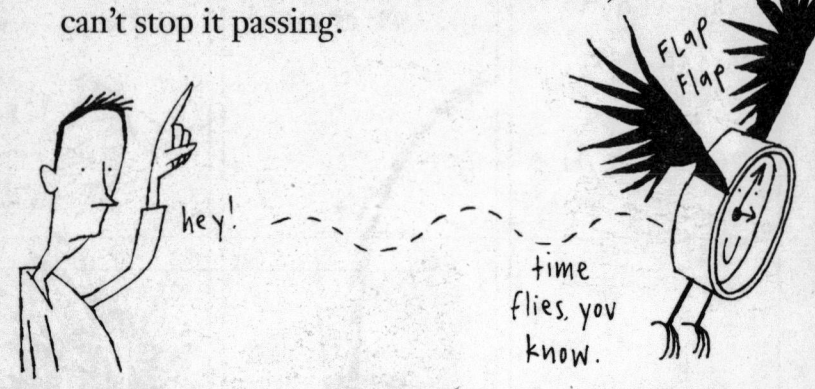

FLAP
FLAP

hey!

time flies, you know.

Time passes at a rate of 60 seconds every minute, 60 minutes every hour, 24 hours every day, every day of your life. And it always goes in the same direction.

Once you've painted a picture, you can't unpaint it again.

OH.

what a pity –

ART CRITIC →

Once something has been eaten, it can't be uneaten

Help! I am about to become fish food.

I wouldn't mind eating this all over again.

MUNCH MUNCH

Time is always passing and can't be held back or altered. Things that have happened can't be 'unhappened'.

What's done is done.

are you sure? this was really expensive.

CREAM STOPS AGEING

Time through history

People didn't realise that time is all about things wearing out until the 19th century. Before then, most ideas about time were circular.

This is hardly surprising, because nature seems to go round in circles. Day and night, the phases of the moon and the changing seasons are all natural cycles.

I'm a natural cyclist –

Understanding the cycle of the seasons helped prehistoric hunters to know where migrating herds of animals would be at different times.

When people started growing food to eat nearly 10,000 years ago, they needed to study the seasons to work out the best time to sow seeds.

But people needed to find out how to measure time more accurately.

The simplest kind of clock is a sundial, and the simplest sundial is just a stick stuck in the ground.

The shadow of the stick moves around the stick as the Sun moves across the sky.

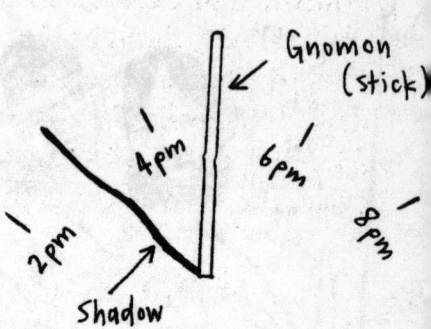

Gnomon (stick)

4pm

6pm

8pm

2pm

Shadow

And they say nothing ever happens round here.

More elaborate sundials can be used to tell the time very accurately...

shadow

gnomon

...but only if the Sun is shining!

dial

The idea of circular time was so powerful that in many cultures people thought that history literally repeats itself. The Mayan civilization, which flourished in Central America between 600 AD and 900 AD, thought that time could be divided up into a series of cycles. These cycles lasted 20 days, 360 days, 7,200 days, 144,000 days and 23,040,000,000 days. At the end of the longest cycle, the Universe was thought to be reborn.

HAPPY NEW UNIVERSE!

WHOOPEE

YEE-HA

FUNKY

YIPEE

WHIZZO

GET DOWN

GROOVY

YAHOO

HOOEE

One of the earliest ways to tell the time when the Sun wasn't shining was with a water clock. Water clocks were used until quite recently by Native Americans and in North Africa.

The water clock container has a hole in it through which water escapes at a more or less steady rate.

A float in the clock makes it easy to see how far the level has dropped.

But water clocks aren't perfect. Once the water level drops, the water trickles out more slowly. This means that a water clock can't measure time evenly.

At the third drip the time will be 11.15 precisely

The Romans solved this problem by inventing a water clock which was constantly topped up with water from a very large reservoir.

You can also measure time using fire. A simple candle marked with evenly spaced lines works as a clock, provided the flame keeps burning.

A better kind of fire clock was invented by the Chinese, thousands of years ago.

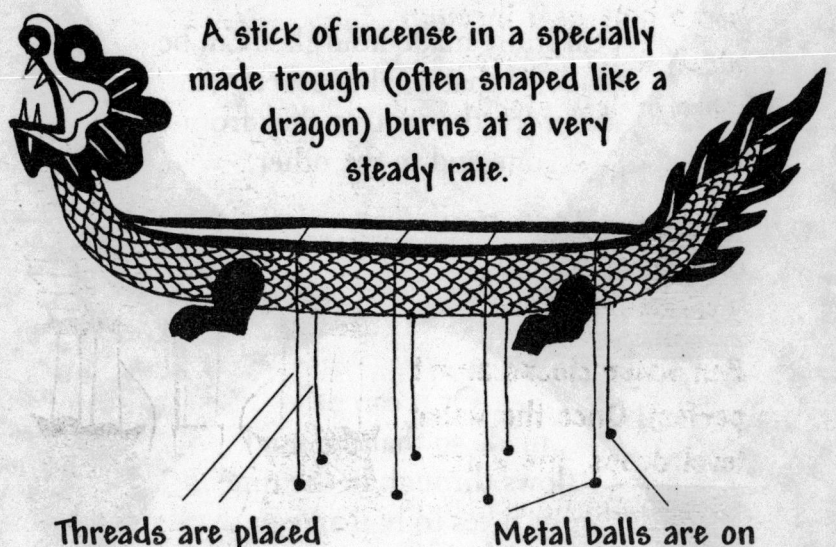

A stick of incense in a specially made trough (often shaped like a dragon) burns at a very steady rate.

Threads are placed at even distances along the stick

Metal balls are on the ends of the dangling threads.

plink

plink

plink

OOYAH

As each thread burns through the balls drop onto a metal tray striking the hours.

This kind of fire clock was still being used in the 19th century.

25

The hourglass is one of the oldest forms of clock and is still sometimes used today. It is just a double-ended container, partly filled with fine sand. The speed at which the sand flows through the hole in the middle depends on the width of the hole.

A carefully made hourglass can be made so that it takes exactly one hour for the sand to flow from one end to the other.

Or it can be made so that the sand flows through in the time it takes to boil an egg.

But if an hourglass was your only way of telling the time, you would have to keep watching it and turning it over every time all the sand had flowed through, and making a note of every hour that passed. You'd have to stay up all night!

the hours aren't good, but at least it's steady work. —

The first mechanical clocks that looked a bit like modern clocks were invented more than 600 years ago. They were very large machines, built in towers. They were driven by weights falling to the ground, attached by ropes to a system of cogs and pulleys.

1335 – The first public clock that struck the hours was built in Milan, Italy.

1386 – The oldest surviving clock was built. It is kept at Salisbury Cathedral.

HELP!

1389 – A clock was built in Rouen, France with a mechanism for chiming every quarter hour – it is still there today!

These early clocks looked really impressive but they did not keep very accurate time.

27

The first portable clocks were invented by a German locksmith, Peter Henlein, at the beginning of the 16th century. These clocks were driven by a spring. Henlein's clock didn't have a minute hand, only a hand to mark the hours.

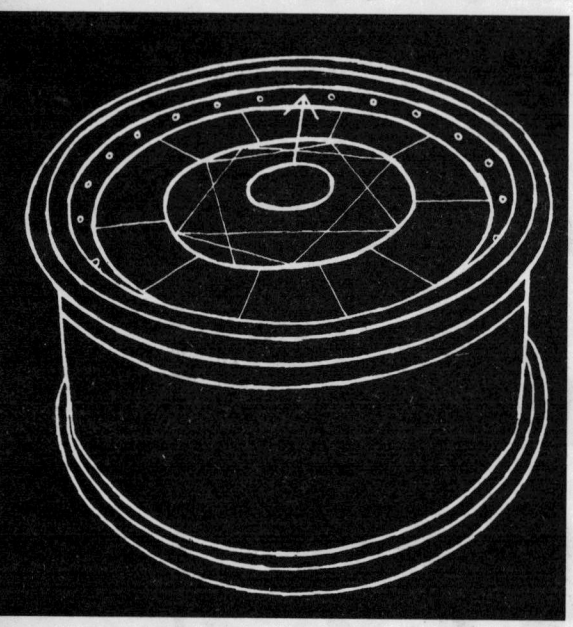

The spring-driven mechanism became known as 'clockwork'.

The minute hand wasn't invented until 1670.

But how could people tell the time when they went out? The first watches were made soon after Henlein invented the clockwork clock.

The watches were more than 10 cm across and 7 cm thick, but they could be carried around in the hand without stopping. Until 1580, they were made of iron - so you had to be strong to carry one.

WHEEZE

Around 1580, the great Italian scientist Galileo Galilei made a major breakthrough in clock technology. He got the idea when he looked up at a swinging chandelier and realised that the time it takes for a pendulum to swing once is always the same, whether it swings through a short arc or a wide arc.

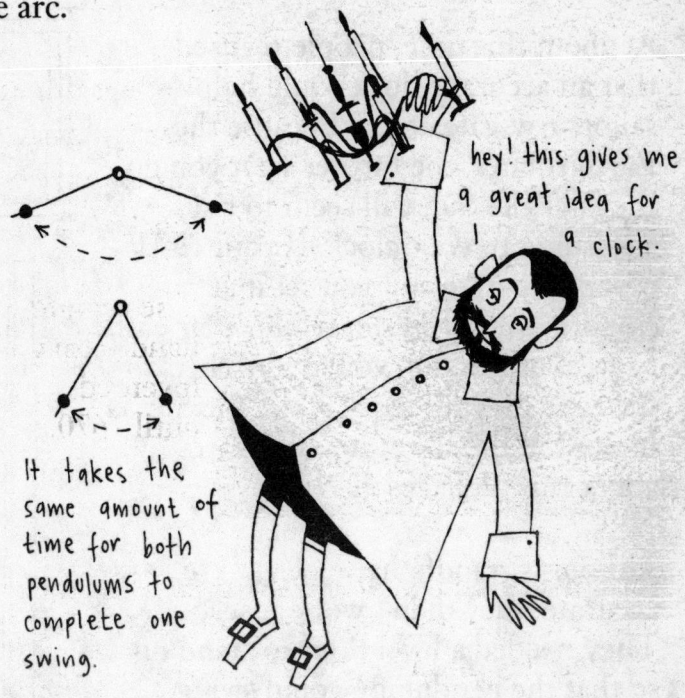

hey! this gives me a great idea for a clock.

It takes the same amount of time for both pendulums to complete one swing.

Galileo used this idea to develop the first pendulum clock. But it didn't work very well.

In 1657, the Dutch scientist Christiaan Huygens improved on Galileo's idea and became the first person to make a practical pendulum clock. A year later, pendulum clocks in church towers were a common sight across Holland. At last, ordinary people had a way of telling the time accurately.

In 1670, William Clement invented a clock with a long pendulum that could tick off the seconds accurately. These long clocks were soon cased in a wooden box to stop the pendulum getting knocked.

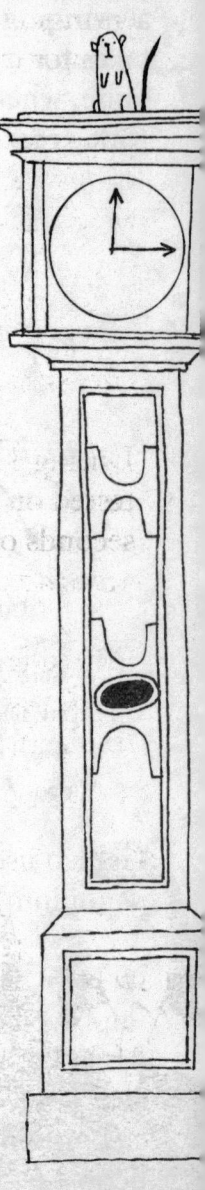

They were cal
'grandfathe
clocks.

At about this time, people realised that an accurate clock could help sailors navigate at sea. Because the Earth rotates, the further west you go, the later the Sun will seem to rise, according to your clock. If your clock is very accurate and you set it at London time, you can tell how far east or west of London you are by checking the time on your clock when the Sun is highest in the sky at noon. (More about this on pages 42-43.)

Although grandfather clocks were very accurate, they didn't work at sea. They needed a level floor to stand on so that the pendulum would swing properly.

where are we?

No idea

HMS. CLUELESS

Without an accurate clock, navigation was rather hit and miss. So, to solve the problem, in 1714 the British government offered a prize of £20,000 (an enormous sum at that time) to anyone who could find a way to keep time accurately at sea.

John Harrison, an English clockmaker, built a series of very accurate clocks (called **chronometers**) to try to win the prize.

His first design stood 63 cm high and weighed 34 kilos. But he found that the smaller he made his chronometer, the better it kept time.

During 1761 and 1762 Harrison's chronometer was tested on a voyage to the West Indies. It lost just 5.2 seconds on the whole journey, making it the most accurate chronometer yet produced.

The judges couldn't believe that the most accurate clock was so small. But they had to give the prize to Harrison.

UNBELIEVABLE

THIS IS THE ONE

By the end of the 19th century, clocks and watches that kept accurate time were available for anybody who could afford to buy them. People started to travel further to work and accurate timekeeping became more and more important to everyone as the 20th century progressed.

and what time do you call this?

9.15 and twenty two seconds.

Today, digital watches that keep time even more accurately than Harrison's chronometer are so cheap to make that they are sometimes given away free.

And as a special incentive to signing your soul away we are giving you a free watch.

COOL

Your watch is probably accurate enough for your everyday needs, but **atomic clocks** are incredibly accurate.

An atomic clock measures time from flashes of radio waves produced by atoms of a metal called cesium. An atomic clock weighing 30 kilos (lighter than Harrison's first chronometer!) would lose or gain no more than 1 second every 3 million years.

oooh

The world's time is kept by the Bureau International de l'Heure in Paris. It uses an average from 80 atomic clocks in 24 countries and sends out signals accurate to one millisecond. This is the time used for sending out the time pips on the radio.

The most accurate clock in the Universe is a star.

When some stars die, they shrink down into a tiny ball. The Sun is about a million times bigger than the Earth. But these dead stars contain as much matter as there is in the Sun, squeezed into a ball only 10 km across - about as big as a large mountain.

All stars rotate. When a dying star shrinks, it spins faster and faster, just as ice skaters can spin faster by pulling in their arms.

A.

B.

I'm seeing stars.

As star spins on its axis it emits radio waves.

When a star shrinks from the size of the Sun to a ball 10 km across, it ends up spinning hundreds of times every second.

Some of these stars radiate energy out into space. They are called **pulsars**. As the star spins, energy beams flick round and round like a lighthouse beam. The flicks of radio energy can be detected on Earth, using radio telescopes.

Radio waves emitted from spinning star. Picked up by Radio telescope.

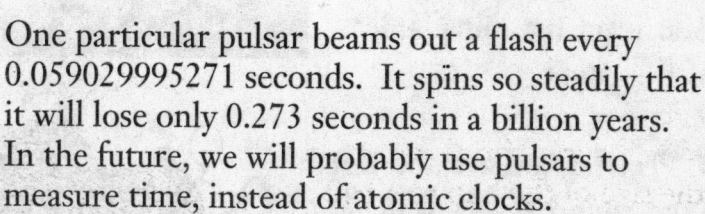

One particular pulsar beams out a flash every 0.059029995271 seconds. It spins so steadily that it will lose only 0.273 seconds in a billion years. In the future, we will probably use pulsars to measure time, instead of atomic clocks.

Pulsars were first detected by two British astronomers, Jocelyn Bell and Antony Hewish.

That's how people through history have measured time during each day. But what about measuring longer periods of time, like a month or a year?

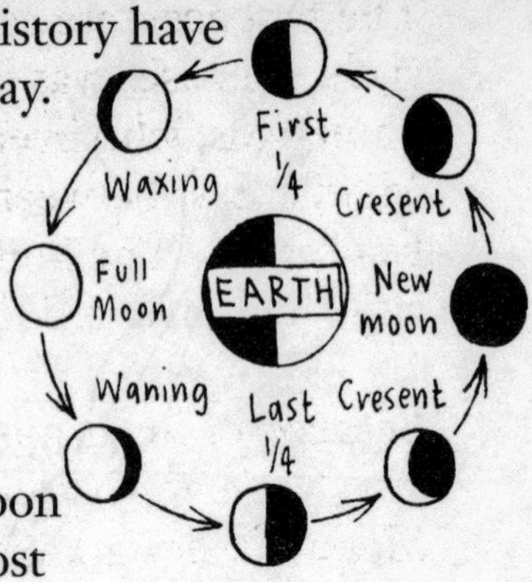

The diagram labels: Waxing, First ¼, Cresent, Full Moon, EARTH, New moon, Waning, Last Cresent, ¼

The first fairly accurate calendars were based on the phases of the Moon. The Moon goes round the Earth in almost exactly 29.5 days. As it moves, it is lit up by the Sun. This makes it go through a cycle of phases roughly every four weeks.

You can see how this works if you have a football, a friend, and a torch.

1. In a dark room, hold the football out at arm's length to represent the moon.

2. Get the friend to shine the torch to represent the Sun from the other side of the room.

CLICK

3. Pretend you are the Earth. Turn round slowly, watching the football.

-WOW.

It's my turn. give it to me.

As you turn, the pattern of shadow on the football will go through the same phases as the Moon.

The first accurate calendar based on the Moon's cycle of phases was developed by the Ancient Sumerians, who lived about 5,000 years ago in the Middle East between the rivers Tigris and Euphrates. The Sumerians also built the first cities and invented the wheel!

Because 12 lunar months add up to almost 11 days less than a year, calendars based only on the Moon's cycles gradually get out of step with the seasons. So, if you celebrated your 10th birthday in midsummer, by the time you were 25, your birthday would be in the middle of winter! This got to be such a problem that something needed to be done.

Something's changed.

I am 25

10

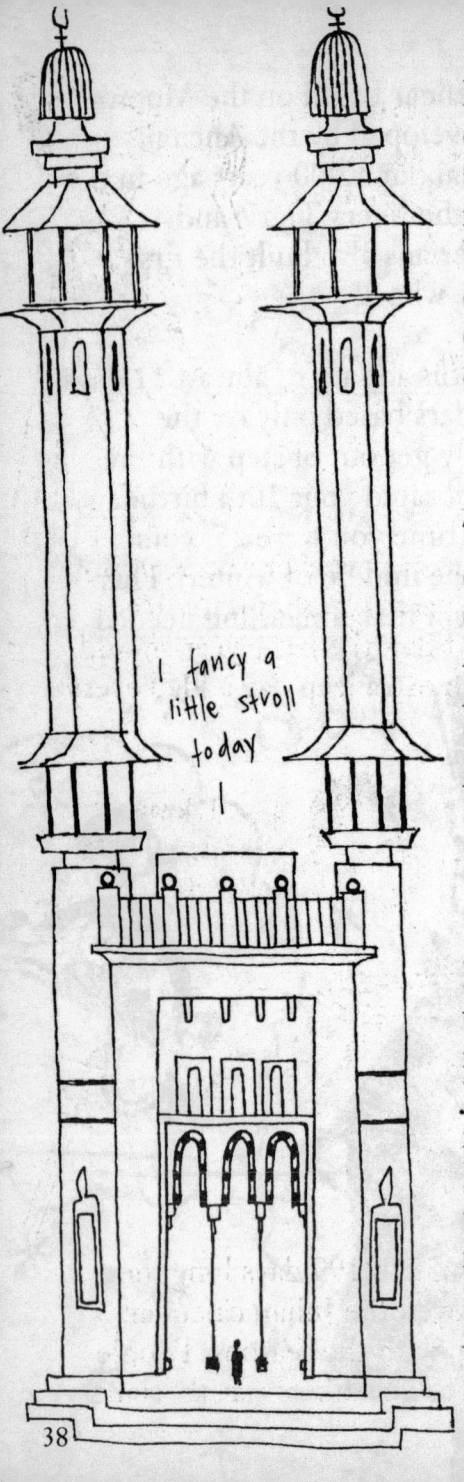

I fancy a little stroll today

In 380 BC, the Jewish calendar developed an accurate system of 12 months alternating between 29 and 30 days in length, with an occasional leap (extra) day and leap month.

The Muslim lunar calendar measures dates from 15 July 622 AD, the day Mohammed set out from Mecca to Medina.

Early Roman calendars were also based on the month, but, in 46 BC, Julius Caesar introduced a new Roman calendar, on the advice of the mathematician Sosigenes of Alexandria.

This new Julian calendar was based on the year, not the month. Because one year lasts about 365 1/4 days, Sosigenes proposed that the basic year should be 365 days long, with an extra leap day added every four years.

But the year is actually 365.242199 days long, not exactly 365.25 days. So even the Julian calendar eventually got out of step with the seasons. People kept on working at ways to get things exactly right.

Sosigenes may have been a brilliant mathematician, but like the rest of the Romans he made a basic error which was not to be corrected for another 1600 years.

A year is the time it takes for the Earth to travel once round the Sun. But this idea was not generally accepted until the 17th century. Because the Sun appears to move across the sky, most people thought that the Sun went round the Earth and the Earth stayed still.

The German astronomer Johannes Kepler (1571-1630) showed that all the planets, including the Earth, move around the Sun in elliptical orbits. This was a revolutionary idea which changed the way people saw the Universe and our place in it. The Earth was no longer at the centre of everything!

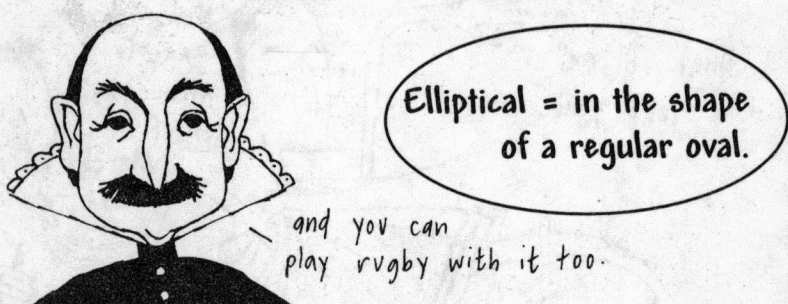

Elliptical = in the shape of a regular oval.

and you can play rugby with it too.

For centuries, people had tried to make sense of the way the planets seemed to wander among the stars in strange, looping orbits. (The word 'planet' comes from the Greek word for 'wanderer'.) Kepler pointed out that our view of the other planets is influenced by the fact that our own planet is also moving.

In 1582, Pope Gregory XIII introduced the Gregorian calendar. This was very like the Julian system, but the leap day was to be skipped every centennial year (1600, 1700 and so on), but kept for millennial years (1000, 2000 etc). This is the calender we still use today.

So the year 1900 was not a leap year, but 2000 will be.

New Year 1900   **New Year 2000**

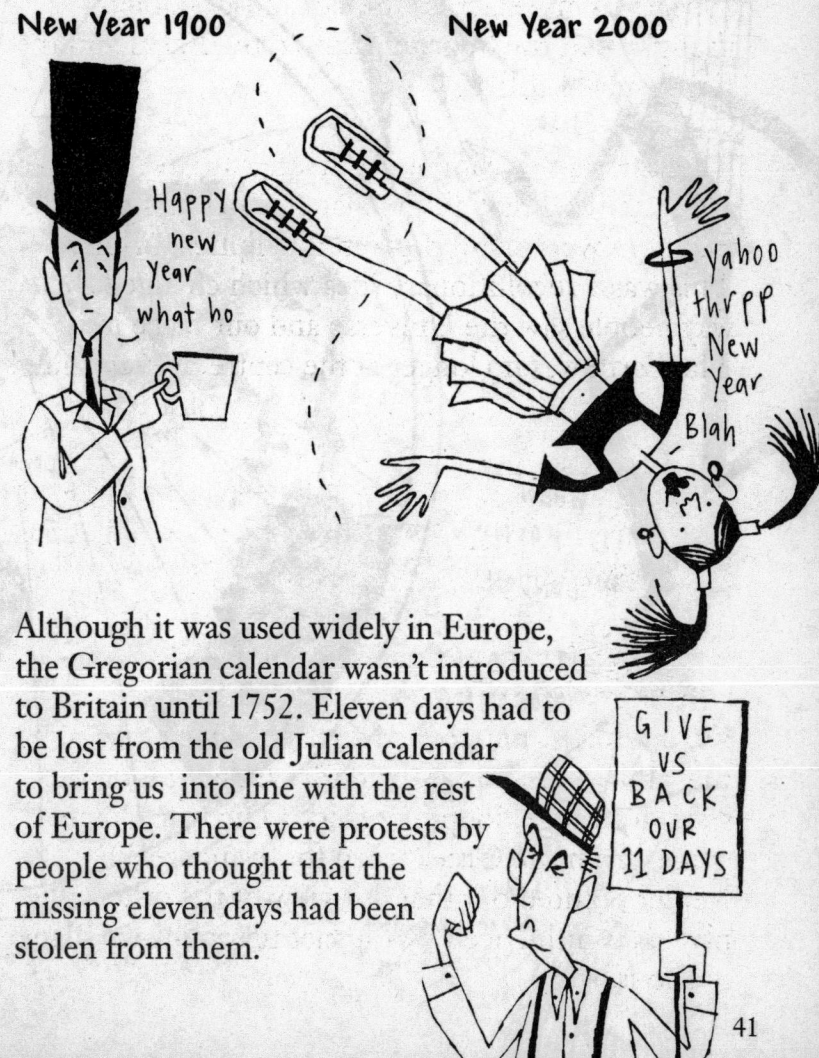

Happy new Year what ho

Yahoo thrpp New Year Blah

Although it was used widely in Europe, the Gregorian calendar wasn't introduced to Britain until 1752. Eleven days had to be lost from the old Julian calendar to bring us into line with the rest of Europe. There were protests by people who thought that the missing eleven days had been stolen from them.

GIVE VS BACK OVR 11 DAYS

41

As some very old problems about time were being solved, new ones were turning up!

Bong Bong Bong

I'm late

15° Rotation = 1 hour.

SO WHEN IT'S NOON IN LONDON...

IT'S EARLY MORNING IN NEW YORK...

New York

London

- hey buddy what time do you call this?

one complete rotation of 360° = 24 hours.

Because the Earth rotates on its axis as it travels round the Sun, the time of day depends on where you are. It rotates once in 24 hours. There are 360 degrees in a circle, so every hour the Earth spins in a day corresponds to 15 degrees of rotation.

Moving east or west by 15 degrees changes the local time (by the Sun) by one hour.

And even if you live in Bristol - roughly $2\frac{1}{2}$ degrees west of London - noon will happen about 10 minutes later than in London.

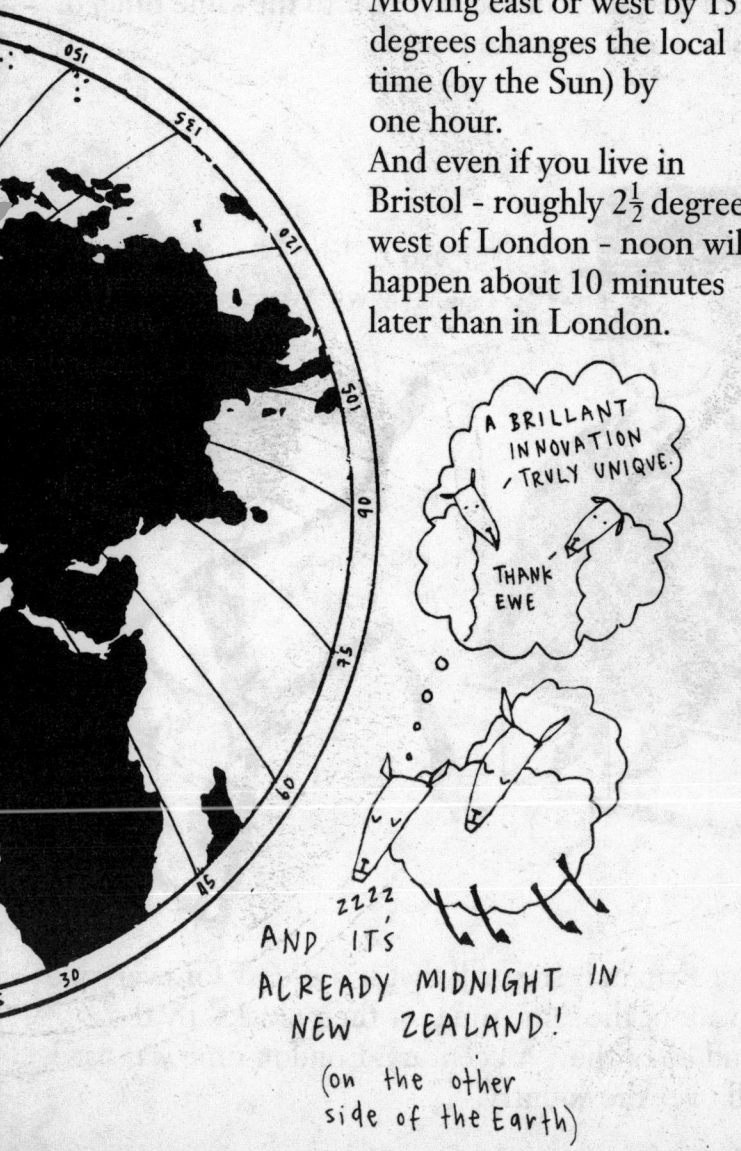

A BRILLANT INNOVATION - TRULY UNIQUE.

THANK EWE

ZZZZ

AND IT'S ALREADY MIDNIGHT IN NEW ZEALAND!

(on the other side of the Earth)

Before the 19th century, nobody except sailors bothered much about these time differences. The only time that mattered was the time by the Sun - your own local time. But when railways were introduced, everybody in the country had to make sure that their clocks were set to the same time, or they would miss the trains.

But Britain is so small that it was easy for everyone to adopt the same time for their clocks. By the middle of the 19th century, London time was used all over the country.

America is too big to peg time to one main city. In 1869 an American schoolteacher called Charles Dowd suggested setting up **time zones**, in which all clocks and watches are set to the same time. The idea was adopted in 1883 by Canadian and US railroads.

In 1884 an international conference held in Washington DC decided that the meridian passing through the observatory in Greenwich, London would be the prime meridian.

A line of longitude is an imaginary line running right around the Earth, over the Poles.
A meridian is one half of a line of longitude, from the North Pole to the South Pole.

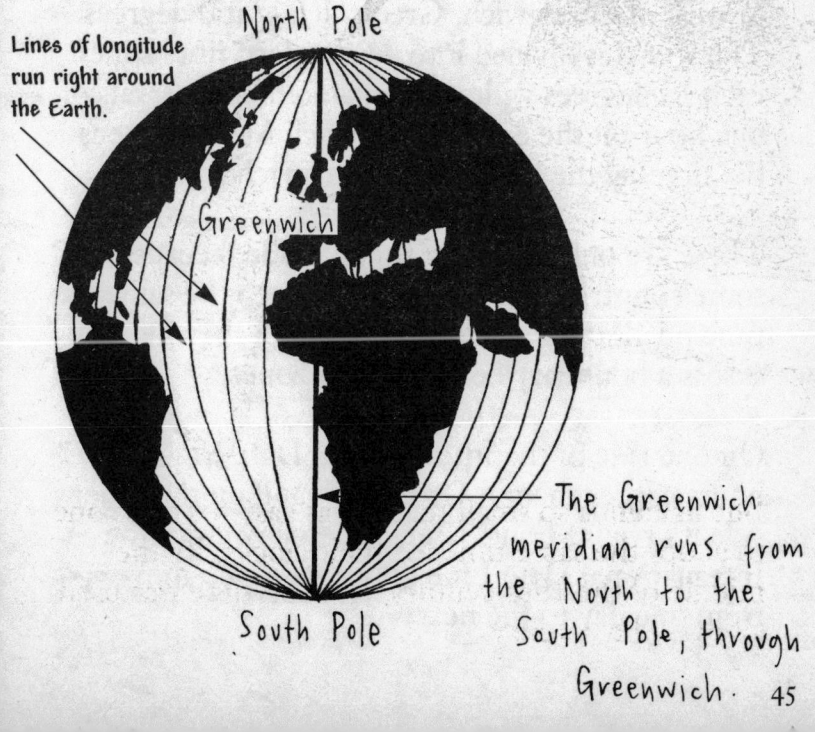

Lines of longitude run right around the Earth.

North Pole

Greenwich

South Pole

The Greenwich meridian runs from the North to the South Pole, through Greenwich. 45

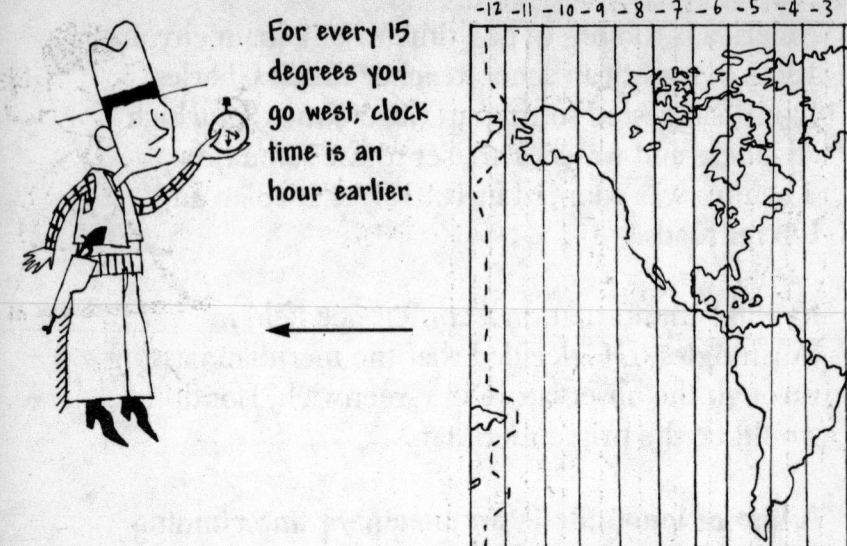

For every 15 degrees you go west, clock time is an hour earlier.

International Date Line 180°

All longitudes since 1884 have been measured east or west of Greenwich. Greenwich is at 0 degrees. The world is divided into 24 standard time zones, each 15 degrees wide and separated by intervals of one hour on the clock. Greenwich Mean Time is the time by the Sun at the Greenwich meridian.

These are only used as a rough guide, because some countries and states like to keep the same time on all their clocks, even though they lie across a boundary between time zones.

On one side of the International Date Line it is 12 hours earlier than in Greenwich and on the other side it's twelve hours later. When you cross the International Date Line going west, you move from one day to the next.

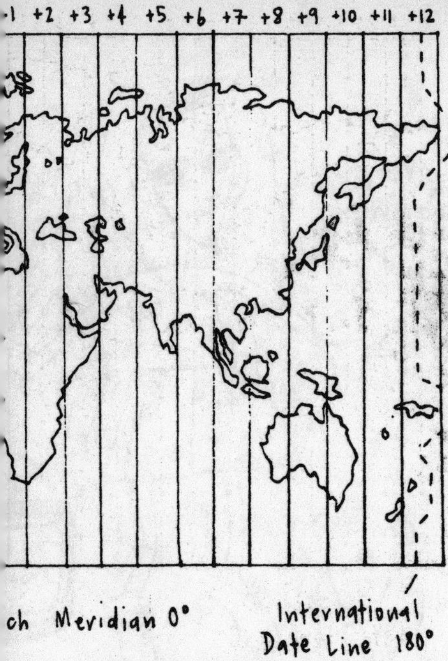

For every 15 degrees you go east, clock time is an hour later.

ch Meridian 0°

International Date Line 180°

If you cross the Line going east, you go back to yesterday, so you could end up having two Christmas days in a row!

Don't even joke — about that.

The Date Line some times zig-zags to make sure that it is the same day everywhere in a particular country. But mostly it follows the 180 degree meridian through the Pacific Ocean.

If you travel to the other side of the Earth, it's not just the time that changes. The seasons are different too.

The annual cycle of the seasons happens because the Earth is tilted over in space, and because it moves around the Sun. Whatever the time of year, the North Pole always points in the same direction in space (roughly towards the Pole star).

When the Sun is on the same side of the Earth as the Pole Star, the Northern Hemisphere leans towards the Sun and gets more light. It's summer! But in the Southern Hemisphere it's dark and wintry. Six months later, everything is the other way around.

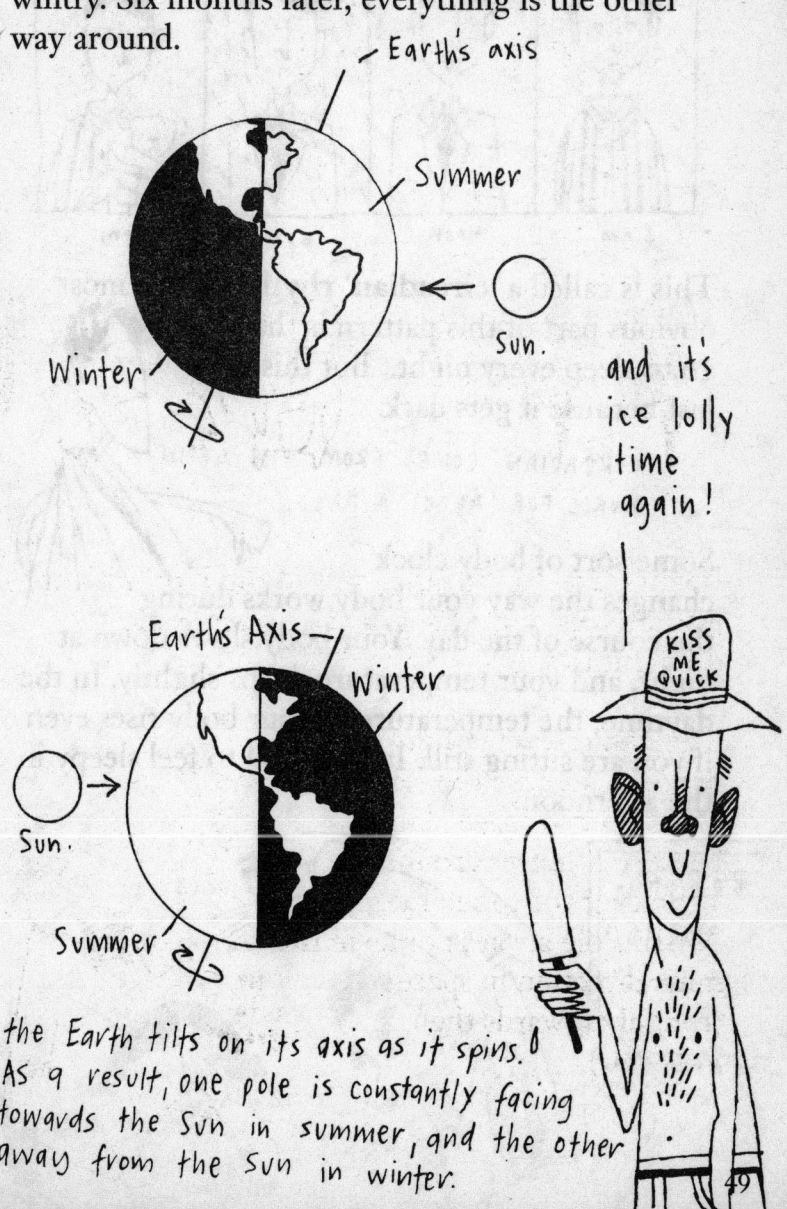

Earth's axis

Summer

Sun.

Winter

and it's ice lolly time again!

Earth's Axis

Winter

Sun.

KISS ME QUICK

Summer

the Earth tilts on its axis as it spins. As a result, one pole is constantly facing towards the Sun in summer, and the other away from the Sun in winter.

49

Life and time

People and many kinds of animals seem to be naturally tuned in to a daily cycle.

8 am   noon   6pm   10pm

This is called a **'circadian' rhythm**. The most obvious part of this pattern is that we go to sleep every night. But this isn't just because it gets dark.

CIRCADIAN COMES FROM THE LATIN WORDS FOR 'ABOUT A DAY'.

Some sort of body clock changes the way your body works during the course of the day. Your body slows down at night, and your temperature drops slightly. In the daytime, the temperature of your body rises even if you are sitting still. It is natural to feel sleepy in the afternoon.

BORING MATHS STUFF

ZZZZ-

GRRR

Human circadian rhythms have been studied in 'caveman' experiments, where people lived in underground bunkers, with no clocks or windows.

HMMMM. You seem to be adjusting rather well Mr. Mole.

They could sleep when they liked, and get up when they liked. After a few days in these conditions, people always settled down into a rhythm about 26 hours long. So in 29 days by the clock, they had experienced only 28 days.

This means that the natural body clock has evolved to run slightly slower than the cycle of day and night. It must be reset each day, either by sunlight or by the alarm clock that wakes you up.

BED TIME. NOW.

I want to reset my body clock with a remote control.

51

Sleep is much more complicated than it seems.

Newborn babies sleep for about 16 hours a day

SNORE

16 year olds need about 10 or 11 hours sleep a night.

In your 20s you need only 8 hours

By the time you are 60, 7 hours is enough.

You need even less in old age.

- Now the young 'uns are asleep let's "rock out"

Most people go through four stages of successively deeper sleep, then a fifth stage of lighter sleep in which their eyes move about and they dream. This fifth stage is called **REM sleep**, which stands for Rapid Eye Movement. It takes about 90 minutes to run through all five cycles, and this happens several times in a night.

Nobody can do without sleep. In the 1970s, in one American study, four volunteers each stayed awake for 205 hours (over eight days.) By the time they had been awake for 60 hours they were experiencing hallucinations, but they still kept going.

In another experiment, researchers tried to see how little sleep they could make do with each night. Even with $5\frac{1}{2}$ hours sleep a night, they found that they were too tired to do their work properly.

I just can't seem to get these sheep counted. Yawn.

BEEP
BEEP

DANGER

Some of the people taking part in the experiment tried to knock off half an hour from their nightly sleep each week. They got down to 5 hours, but then had to give up because they fell asleep in the daytime. Working is much more difficult if you don't get enough sleep.

People with insomnia have trouble getting to sleep and staying asleep all through the night. But experiments designed to study how we sleep show that often people don't have as much trouble as they think.

Time seems to pass very slowly when you lie awake worrying about not being asleep, and people often think they have been awake for much longer than they really have.

Scientists at Stanford University in California found that people who had complained of very bad insomnia were actually only awake for about 30 minutes each night.

Real sleep problems are caused when our body clocks get confused by having to be awake when we would normally be asleep.

People working in places like hospitals, airports and factories often have to work night shifts. They have to be alert and active at the time when their body clock says they should be asleep.

Because of all the different jobs that have to be done through the day and night, most people now live by the clock, instead of by the Sun. This change from the natural influence of time on our lives is most noticeable through its effect on our sleep patterns.

Understanding how time affects your body can help with some kinds of sleep problems.

Some people suffer from 'delayed sleep syndrome'. They have trouble getting to sleep early in the night. Because the natural body clock is set at about 26 hours, not 24, it is easier to go to sleep later rather than earlier. So if people suffering from delayed sleep syndrome go to bed three hours later each day for six days, their body clock is usually reset.

and we can sleep normally from then on. Zzzzzzz.

People working night shifts get used to it eventually, although it takes their body clock about a month to adjust. But then they find it hard to wake up in the day. It is much better to stay on night shifts than to switch from night to day and back every couple of weeks.

If you keep changing shifts, you always feel tired.

whooo

When people travel east or west across time zones by air, their body clocks get out of step with local time and they suffer jet lag.

what ho! I feel tip top!

McGROOVEY

zzzz

Jet lag is worse flying east, because sunset happens sooner than your body expects and it is hard to get to sleep. The best way to avoid jet lag when flying east is to get up a bit sooner each day for a few days before the flight. You will naturally go to bed a little earlier as well, so your body clock will be prepared for the jump across time zones you are about to make.

CRASH

Many creatures have a very strong inbuilt clock. Some kinds of birds, fish and butterflies migrate long distances. They probably know when it is time to migrate by the changing length of daylight as the seasons progress.

American Monarch butterflies spend the winter in California. In spring, at the same time each year, they set off north. On the way, generations of butterflies live, lay eggs, and die. Their descendants spend the summer in Canada. The last generation of summer butterflies flies south again to California for the winter.

Some kinds of animals, including tortoises and some bears, can slow down their bodies so much that they do not need to eat during winter. They go to sleep and hibernate for months.

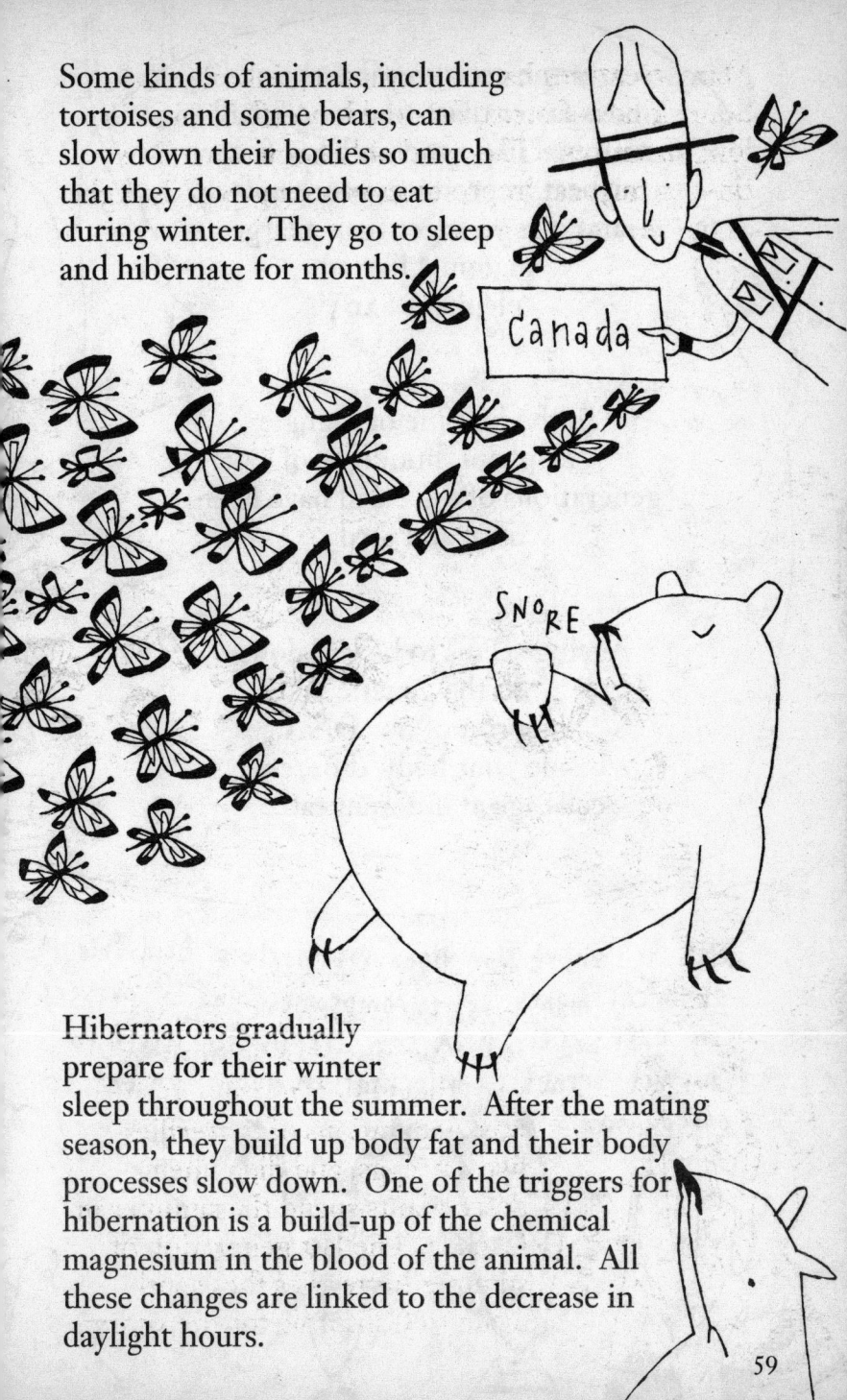

SNORE

Canada

Hibernators gradually prepare for their winter sleep throughout the summer. After the mating season, they build up body fat and their body processes slow down. One of the triggers for hibernation is a build-up of the chemical magnesium in the blood of the animal. All these changes are linked to the decrease in daylight hours.

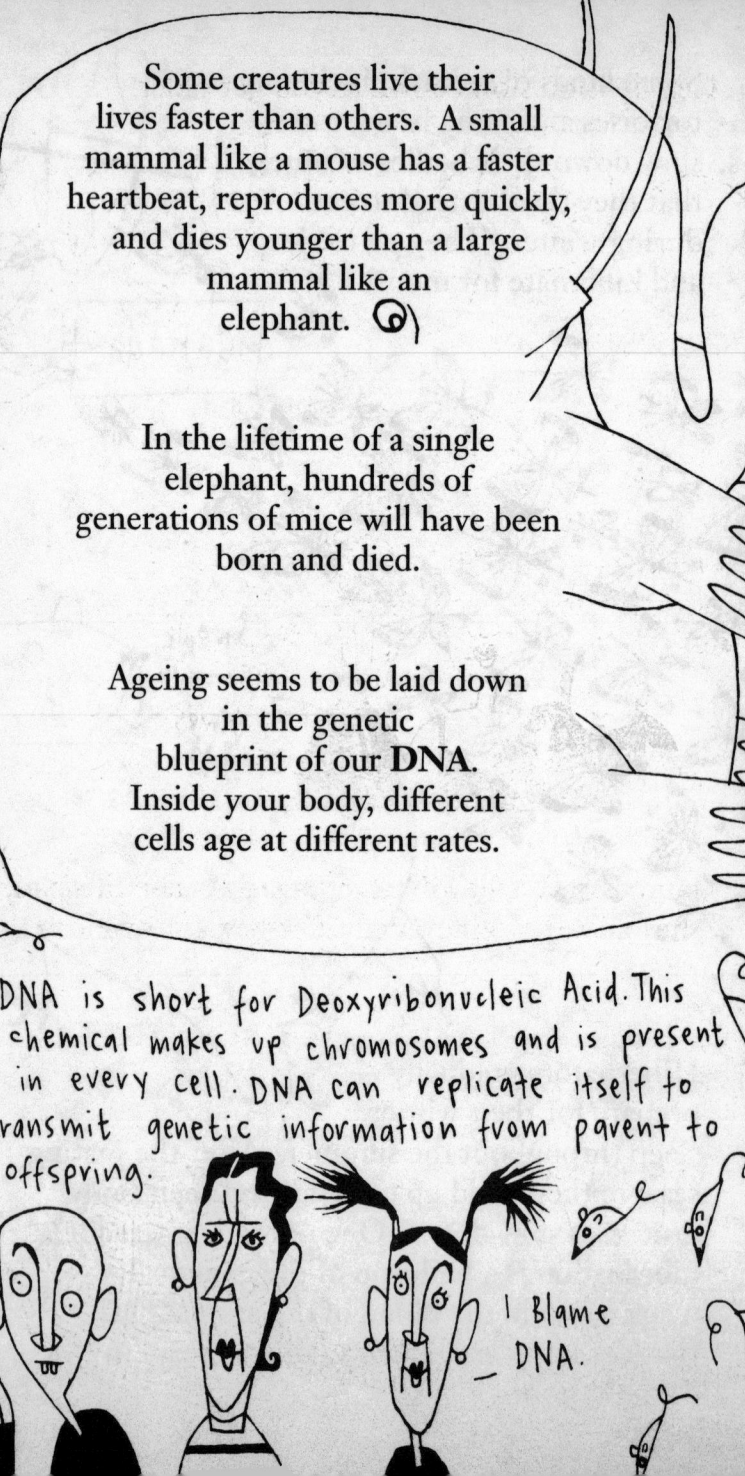

Some creatures live their lives faster than others. A small mammal like a mouse has a faster heartbeat, reproduces more quickly, and dies younger than a large mammal like an elephant.

In the lifetime of a single elephant, hundreds of generations of mice will have been born and died.

Ageing seems to be laid down in the genetic blueprint of our **DNA**. Inside your body, different cells age at different rates.

DNA is short for Deoxyribonucleic Acid. This chemical makes up chromosomes and is present in every cell. DNA can replicate itself to transmit genetic information from parent to offspring.

I Blame DNA.

Cell division slows down as you get older.

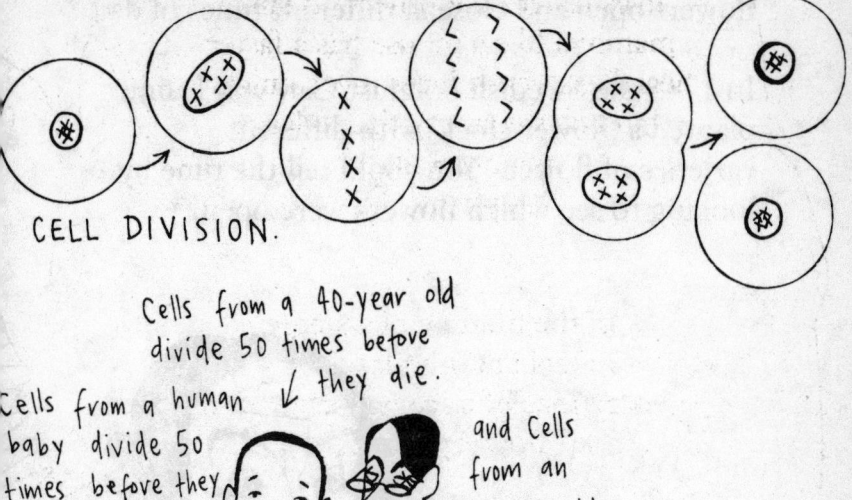

CELL DIVISION.

Cells from a 40-year old divide 50 times before they die.

Cells from a human baby divide 50 times before they die. →

and Cells from an 80-year-old divide only 30 times. ←

Animals have all evolved to have a certain lifespan. They are all programmed to be born, reproduce and die.

Some, like me, live their whole lives in a day.

and some, like me, live over 50 years.

BUZZ

Plants can tell the time in various ways. Some flowers open and close at different times of day.

In 1745 the Swedish botanist Carl von Linne planted a 'flower clock' with different varieties of flower. You could tell the time by looking to see which flowers were open.

the flower watch may be a little harder.

Tree rings are the best known biological calendars. Many trees lay down one growth ring every year. When the tree is felled, you can count the rings to find out how old the tree was, and which year each ring was being laid down.

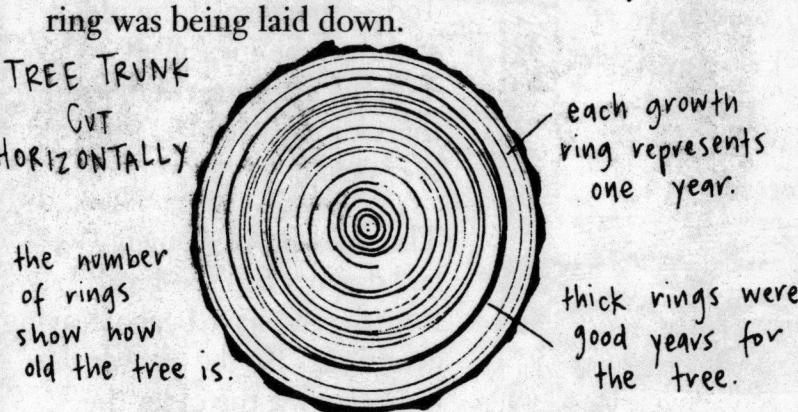

TREE TRUNK CUT HORIZONTALLY

the number of rings show how old the tree is.

each growth ring represents one year.

thick rings were good years for the tree.

Living things also carry a clock they get from the air. Some of the carbon in the carbon dioxide taken up by plants is a radioactive form called carbon-14. Half the carbon-14 'decays' every 5,730 years. So by measuring the amount of carbon-14 in an old bone or piece of wood, archeologists can work out when it was alive. This is called **carbon dating.**

this was a tree when Henry VIII was King —

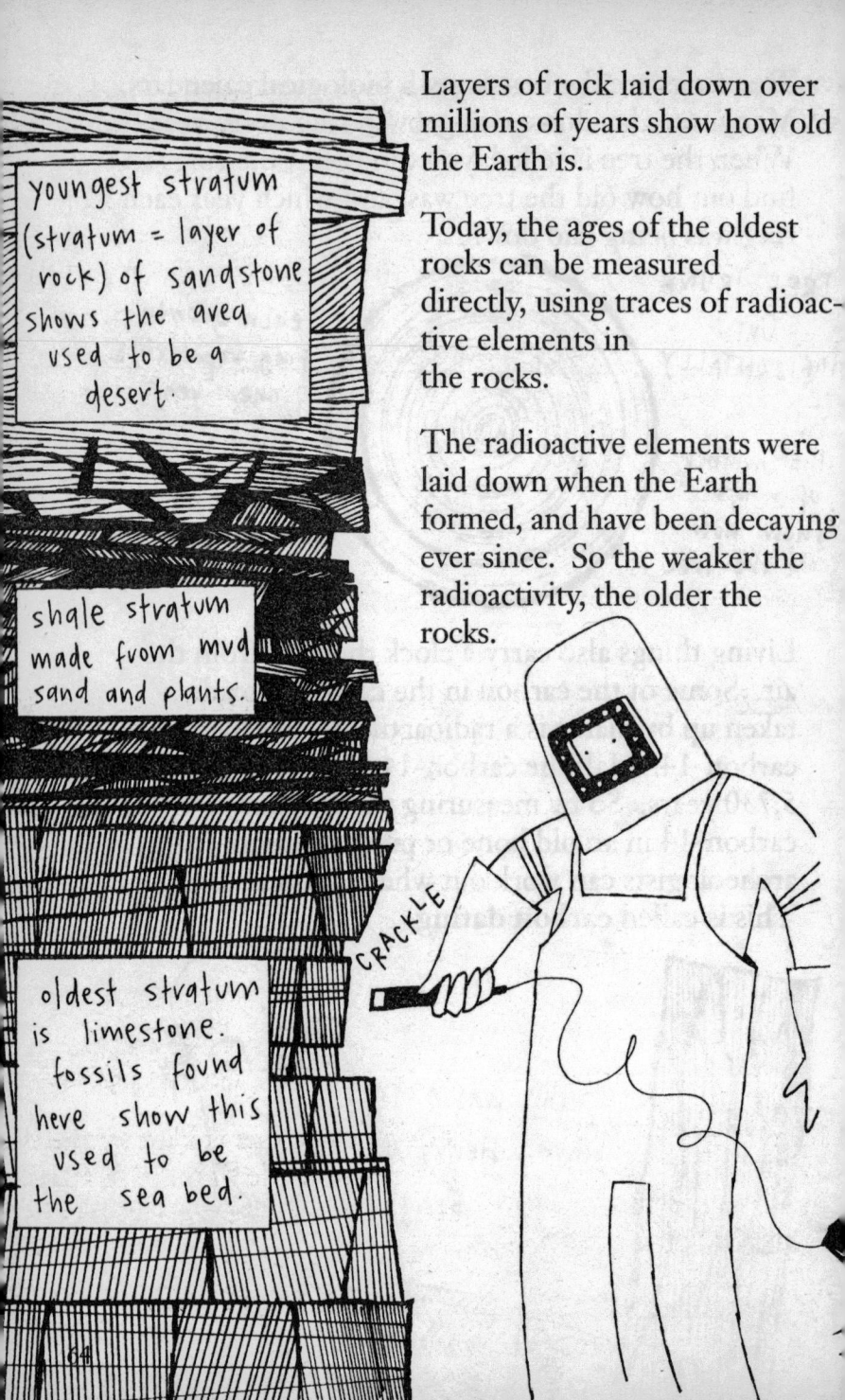

youngest stratum
(stratum = layer of
rock) of sandstone
shows the area
used to be a
desert.

shale stratum
made from mud
sand and plants.

oldest stratum
is limestone.
fossils found
here show this
used to be
the sea bed.

CRACKLE

Layers of rock laid down over millions of years show how old the Earth is.

Today, the ages of the oldest rocks can be measured directly, using traces of radioactive elements in the rocks.

The radioactive elements were laid down when the Earth formed, and have been decaying ever since. So the weaker the radioactivity, the older the rocks.

Two hundred years ago, geologists realised that the Earth must be very old...

it's much older than you think.

Pioneers such as Charles Lyell (1797–1875) pointed out that immense stretches of time must have passed for mountain ranges to have been pushed up by volcanic activity, then ground down by erosion and covered by new layers of rock, which we see in the strata (rock layers) today.

Fossils preserved in the rocks also indicate the passage of time. Sometimes, when living things die, they fall into soft mud and get covered by layers of sediment. The remains are turned to stone and preserved. Very many millions of years would be needed for all the creatures found in different layers of the fossil record to have lived out their lives, one after the other.

fish

sea scorpion

trilobite

tree

Evolution works by the build-up of small changes in individuals from one generation to the next.

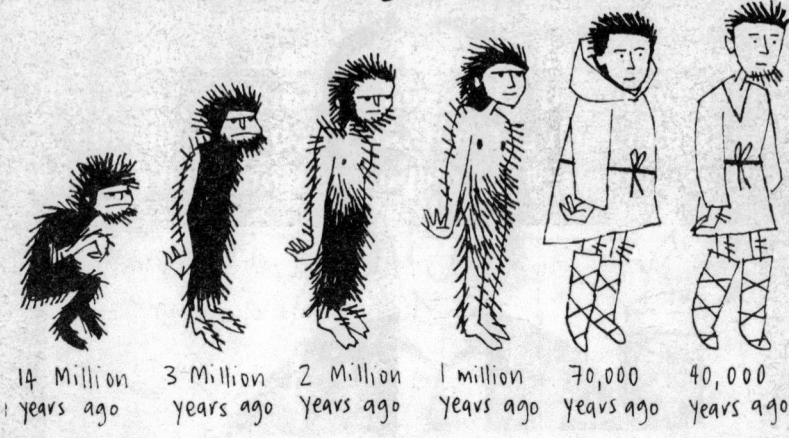

14 Million years ago 3 Million years ago 2 Million years ago 1 million years ago 70,000 years ago 40,000 years ago

Millions

Billions

Biologist Charles Darwin (1809-82) realised that this would require an enormous span of Earth history. When Darwin was alive, astronomers thought that the Sun and the Earth were no more than a few million years old. But geologists studying rocks and fossils agreed with Darwin that the Earth must be *billions* of years old.

Darwin was correct: the Sun has been around for billions of years.
(More about this on page 72.)

RASP
told you so.

How long would it take to turn an elephant into a mouse? If, for some reason like a change in climate or food, smaller elephants were favoured by evolution, and the change took 12,000 generations, the differences would be too small to notice in each generation. But in only 60,000 years, mouse-sized elephants would have evolved.

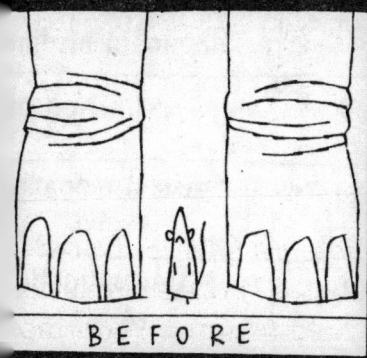

BEFORE

don't even think about climbing a grass stalk.

AFTER

60,000 years is less than the interval between the laying down of successive rock strata. So geologists might find full-size elephant fossils in one layer, and mouse-sized elephant fossils in the next, without ever seeing fossils from the 60,000 years in which the changeover happened!

Eon	Era	Period		Million years ago	Major Evolutionary Events
Phanerozoic	Cenozoic	NEOGENE		24	Apes evolve
		PALEOCENE		65	Death of the dinosaurs
	Mesozoic	Cretaceous		144	Flowering plants becom dominant on land
		Jurassic		213	Major extinction of life
		Triassic		248	Earliest mammals evolve
	Paleozoic	Permian		286	Major extinction of life
		Carboniferous	Pennsylvanian	320	Earliest reptiles evolve
			Mississipian	360	Vertebrates invade the land
		Devonian		408	Land plants become conspicuous
		Silurian		438	Major extinction of life
		Ordovician		505	Earliest fish evolve
		Cambrian		590	Great diversification of life in the sea
		Precambrian		650	

Era	Period	Million years ago	Epoch	Traditional Period	
Cenozoic	NEOGENE	0.01	Holocene	Quaternary	
		1.8	Pleistocene		Humans evolve
		5	Pliocene	Tertiary	Present ice epoch begins
		24	Miocene		Apes evolve
	PALEOCENE	37	Oligocene		Extinction of many species
		58	Eocene		Monkeys evolve
		65	Paleocene		Mammals diversify
Cretaceous			Cretaceous		

The chart on the left looks back over the big events in evolution over 650 million years, starting at the bottom with early sea creatures and working up to apes at the top. Above is a more detailed view of the most recent periods, up to the evolution of the first humans.

Time and space

Life is constantly
renewed on Earth because
of the energy we get from
the Sun. We seem to have
beaten the Second Law of
Thermodynamics
(see page 8). But this will only
keep going as long as the Sun lasts.

The Sun gets its energy by turning hydrogen atoms into helium atoms. Each time it does so, a tiny bit of matter is turned into energy. Every second, the Sun converts an amount of matter equivalent to the weight of five million elephants into pure energy. The energy escapes and the Sun is that much lighter (and smaller) each second. But the Sun is so big, and has so much hydrogen, that it has been able to burn at this rate for millions of years without changing much.

how long exactly? —

Good question!

The Sun and the Earth have not been around for ever. They were born about 5 billion years ago, when a cloud of gas and dust in space collapsed.

When the cloud collapsed, it was spinning slightly. As the centre of the cloud shrank down to become the Sun, it span faster.

Some of the gas and dust was flung off by the spinning and formed rings around the Sun, like the rings of Saturn.

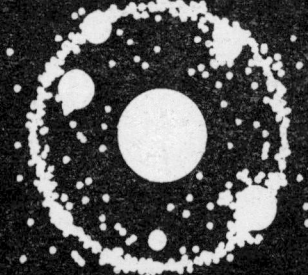

The Earth and the other planets formed when the debris in those rings stuck together in lumps.

The Sun has enough hydrogen fuel to last for another 5 billion years. When it has used up all its hydrogen, it will start to 'burn' helium in a similar way. This will make it even hotter inside and make its atmosphere swell up. It will become a Red Giant star.

When the Sun becomes a Red Giant, its heat will scorch the Earth and make life as we know it impossible. But helium burning will not keep the Sun hot for long. When all its fuel is exhausted, it will shrink down into a white-hot ball about as big as the Earth - a White Dwarf.

the Sun shrinks and no longer gives off heat.

Earth would freeze over

Oh Boy.

The fate of the Sun is to become a cooling cinder a fraction of its original size. But stars that are several times bigger than the Sun end their lives more dramatically - they explode.

These exploding stars are called supernovas. As they explode, they blow huge clouds of material out into space. The gas and dust that makes new stars and planets comes from supernovas.

Everything on Earth (including you!) is made of stuff that has been processed inside stars, blown into space, and then been pulled together by gravity to become part of our Solar System.

So even stars have a kind of life cycle. They are born, live their lives, die, and give way to the next generation.

When the Sun dies, time will not stop, because there will be other stars pouring energy out into the Universe. But the whole Universe will still be wearing out very slowly.

Energy flows out of the Sun and stars. But how did the energy get in there in the first place? How did time begin?

All the stars you can see in the sky are part of a family called the Milky Way Galaxy. Our Sun is one of them - the other stars are all suns in their own right. Even on the darkest night, you can only see a couple of thousand stars. But telescopes show that our Galaxy contains more than a hundred billion stars, spread out in a disk.

Our home in space is a kind of island of stars.

It is so big that light would take 100,000 years to cross the disk, but it is 'only' about 20,000 light years thick. All the stars are orbiting around the centre of the Galaxy.

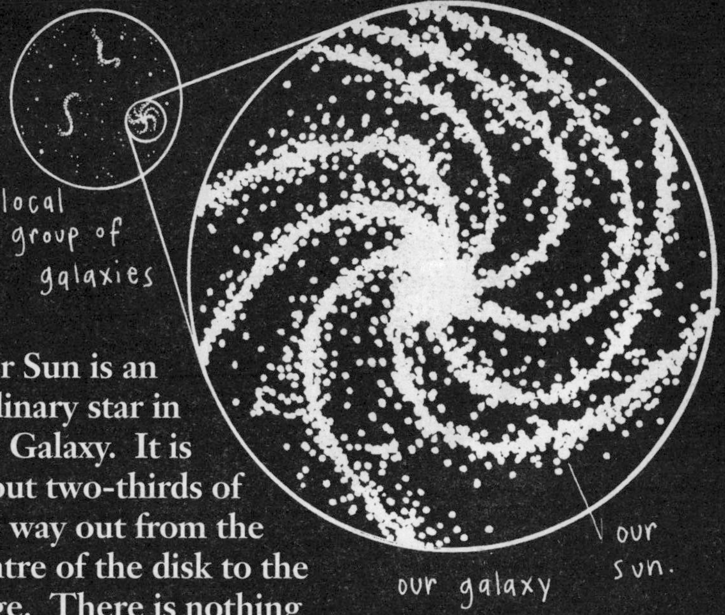

local group of galaxies

our galaxy

our Sun.

Our Sun is an ordinary star in the Galaxy. It is about two-thirds of the way out from the centre of the disk to the edge. There is nothing special about the Sun or its place in the Galaxy. Our Milky Way Galaxy is just one island in space. There are hundreds of millions of other galaxies, beyond the Milky Way. One of them, a galaxy very like our own, can be seen as a fuzzy patch of light in the constellation Andromeda.

The Andromeda galaxy is so far away that light from it takes more than two million years to reach us. Yet it is our nearest large neighbour in space. No other large galaxy is close enough to be seen with the naked eye. Astronomers have detected some galaxies more than ten billion light years away.

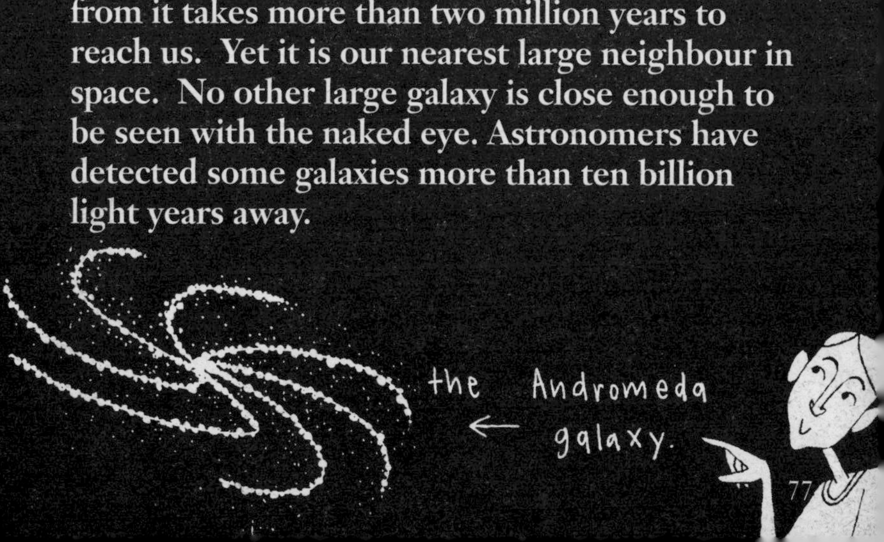

the Andromeda
← galaxy.

Light from the Sun and stars can be split up by a prism (a triangular wedge of glass or plastic) to make a rainbow pattern called the spectrum.

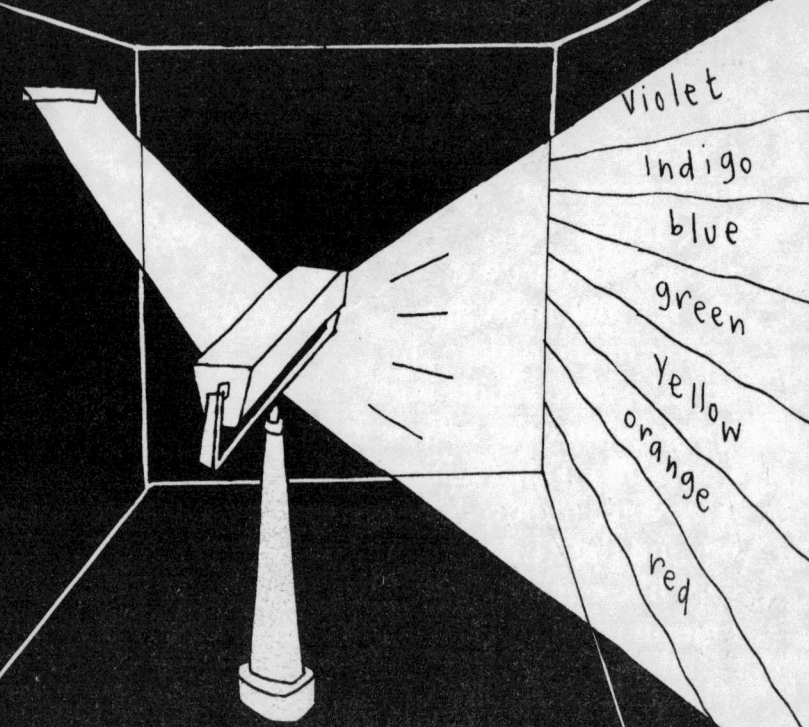

Violet
Indigo
blue
green
yellow
orange
red

This rainbow pattern is marked by dark lines. In the light from distant galaxies, the dark lines are shifted towards the red part of the spectrum. This is called a red shift. It is caused because space has stretched while the light was on its way to us. The stretching of space has stretched the light, moving the lines to the red part.

The further away a galaxy is, the bigger its red shift. The whole Universe is expanding.

It looks as if we are in the middle of the Universe, but we are not.

Imagine a balloon dotted with blobs of paint. If you blow up the balloon to twice its original size, all the paint blobs will move further apart.

If you measure from any blob, you'll see that the other blobs have moved away from it. Imagine that each blob is a galaxy. Whichever galaxy you lived in, it would look to you as if all the other galaxies were moving away from you, and that you were at the centre of the Universe.

The Universe is getting bigger. So it must have been smaller long ago.

Imagine winding time backwards. There must have been a time when all the galaxies touched.

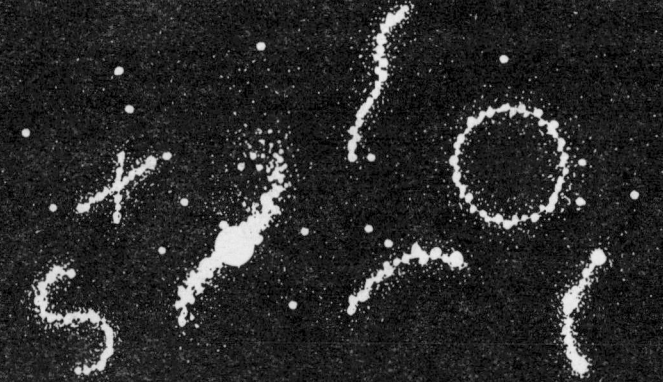

Before that, when all the stars touched.

And, before that, a time when all the atoms in the stars were squashed together.

and before that?

The best explanation for what happened at the beginning is that everything in the Universe came from a tiny, hot fireball. This is known as the

BIG BANG

WOW!

The Universe was born in a Big Bang.

It has been wearing out ever since. Time began in the Big Bang and Entropy started to increase from that moment.

By measuring how fast the Universe is expanding now, astronomers can work out how long it is since the Big Bang created it. They measure how fast the Universe is expanding from the red shift.

BIG BANG

UNIVERSE EXPANDS

PRESENT

Measurements of the red shift show that the Big Bang happened about 15 billion years ago.

What happened before the Big Bang?

15 Billion =

15,000,000,000

Nothing!

The Big Bang was not like a lump of compressed matter exploding into empty space. There was nowhere for the Big Bang to expand into, because space was made in the Big Bang.

There was no before the Big Bang, because time was made in the Big Bang.

The Big Bang is the edge of time, the moment when time began. Time has only existed for 15 billion years.

More about the Big Bang on page 92. But first you have to get your head around **spacetime**...

Space and time seem to be very different things. You can move about anywhere you like in space. But you can only move one way in time, from the past into the future

There are three dimensions of space. You can move forward/backward, left/right, or up/down.

forward back | left right | up / down

There is only one dimension of time. Worse, you can only move in one direction along it. It is like a long, straight road that you have to keep marching along in the same direction.

In 1905, the great scientist Albert Einstein (1879-1955) realised that space and time are connected. And he found that the way space and time look to you depends on how fast you are moving.

In 1907, Hermann Minkowski used geometry to explain what Einstein had already discovered in terms of geometry. Minkowski said that time is a dimension like space, and that space and time together make up the four dimensions of spacetime.

Time is a direction like space, but the time 'direction' is at right angles to all of the space directions.

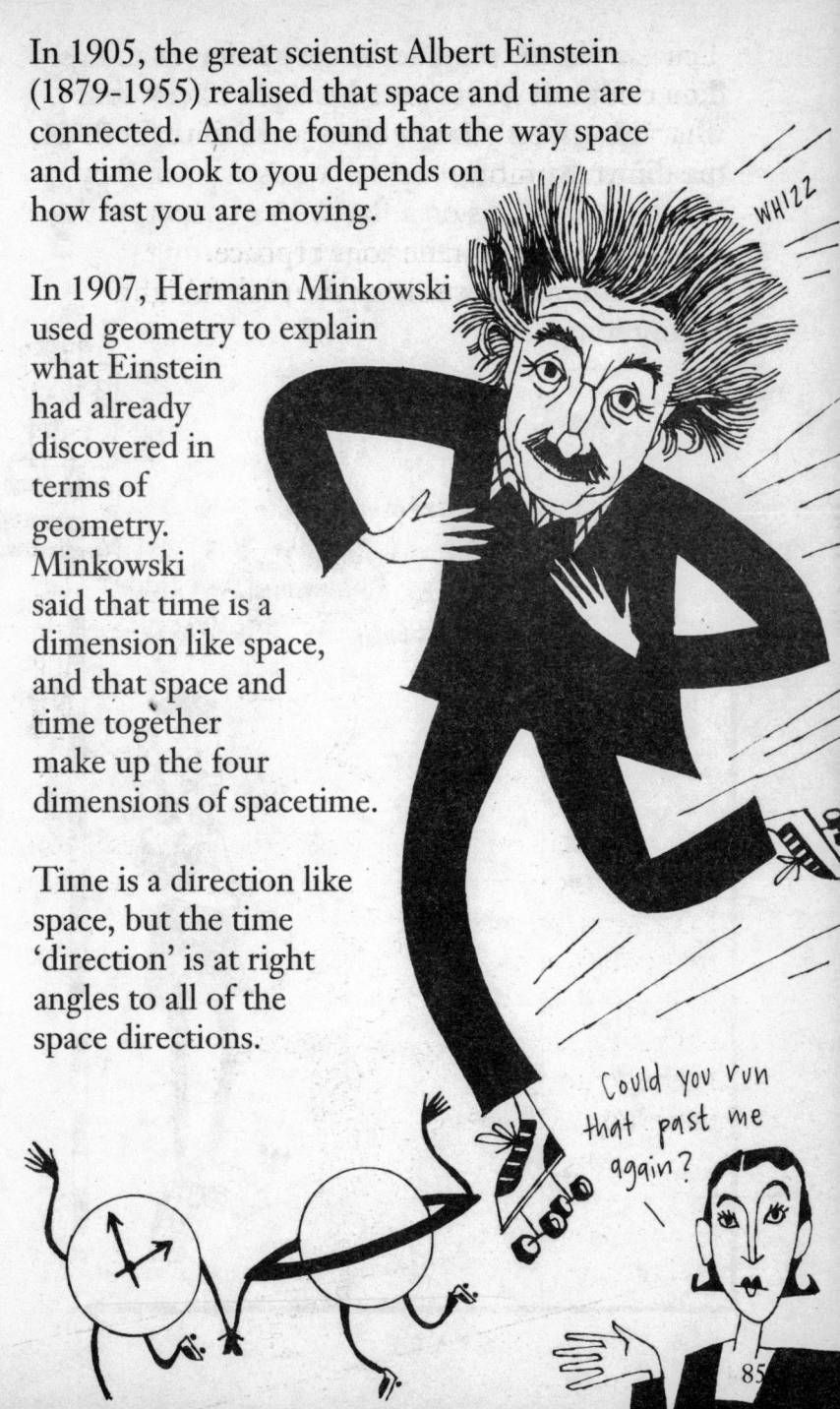

WHIZZ

Could you run that past me again?

85

Time and space together make up the four dimensions of spacetime. It is hard to visualise what this means. So scientists pretend that two of the dimensions of space don't exist. Then they can draw diagrams on a flat sheet of paper, with the direction across the page representing space, and the direction up the page representing time.

IN A SPACETIME DIAGRAM, IF YOU STAND STILL YOU MOVE ONLY THROUGH TIME. SO YOUR HISTORY IS REPRESENTED BY A LINE GOING STRAIGHT UP THE PAGE AS TIME PASSES.

BUS STOP

TIME

tap tap

SPACE

IF YOU MOVE THROUGH SPACE AS WELL, YOU MAKE A WIGGLY LINE IN A SPACETIME DIAGRAM.

SPACE

Anything moving at the speed of light moves diagonally across the diagram, at 45 degrees. Nothing can move faster through space than light.

Einstein said that anybody, anywhere in the Universe, is entitled to say that they are at rest, and to measure all movement relative to themselves. This is called the **Special Theory of Relativity**.

and so at last we can prove the need for a tea-break.

SPECIAL
THEORY of
RELATIVITY.
$E = mc^2$
(energy = matter × light × light)

Einstein's theory says that when an object moves past you, it shrinks a little bit. And when a clock moves relative to you, time runs more slowly for the moving clocks.

did you see that!

crumbs

We don't notice this in everyday life, because the effects are only large enough to notice if something is travelling at close to the speed of light - 300,000 kilometres per second.

All of the predictions of the Special Theory of Relativity have been tested. Scientists can make particles move at very nearly the speed of light in accelerators, like the giant machines at CERN, the European physics research centre near Geneva.

All the experiments show that the Special Theory is correct. Moving objects do shrink, and moving clocks do run slow. Time itself runs more slowly for moving objects.

If you travelled in a space ship moving at almost the speed of light on a journey that lasted a year, when you came back to Earth you would find that, although you were only a year older, decades or centuries had passed back home.

This is a kind of one-way time travel.

I'm afraid we evolved into a higher life form while you were gone.

The way space shrinks and time stretches for moving things is because space and time are connected in spacetime.

Think of a square block of rubber, like an ordinary pencil eraser. One side of the square represents time, the other side (at right angles) represents space.

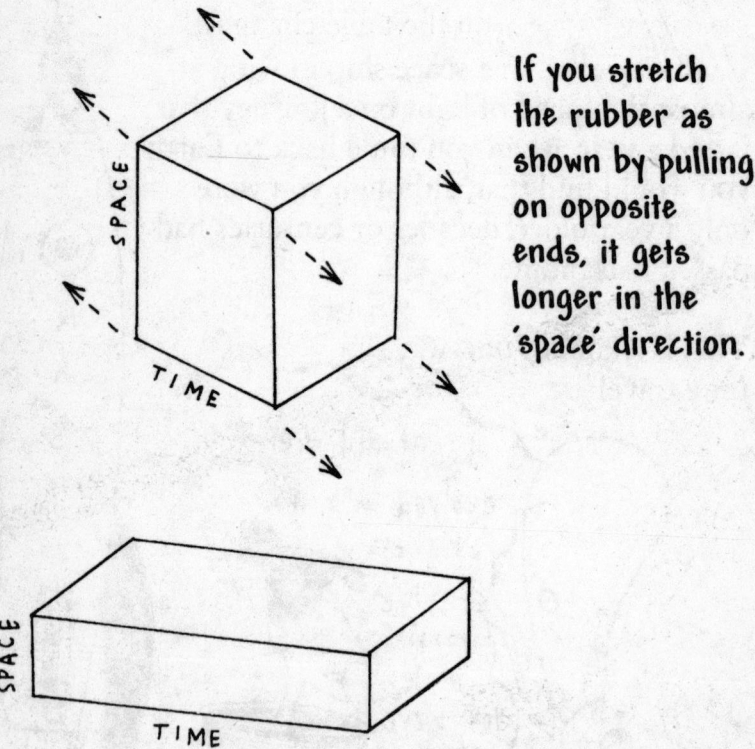

If you stretch the rubber as shown by pulling on opposite ends, it gets longer in the 'space' direction.

But as the rubber stretches, it gets thinner in the 'time' direction.

In spacetime, there is an exact balance between space and time. However things move, a kind of average of their own space and time stays the same.

Another way to think of this is like a shadow.

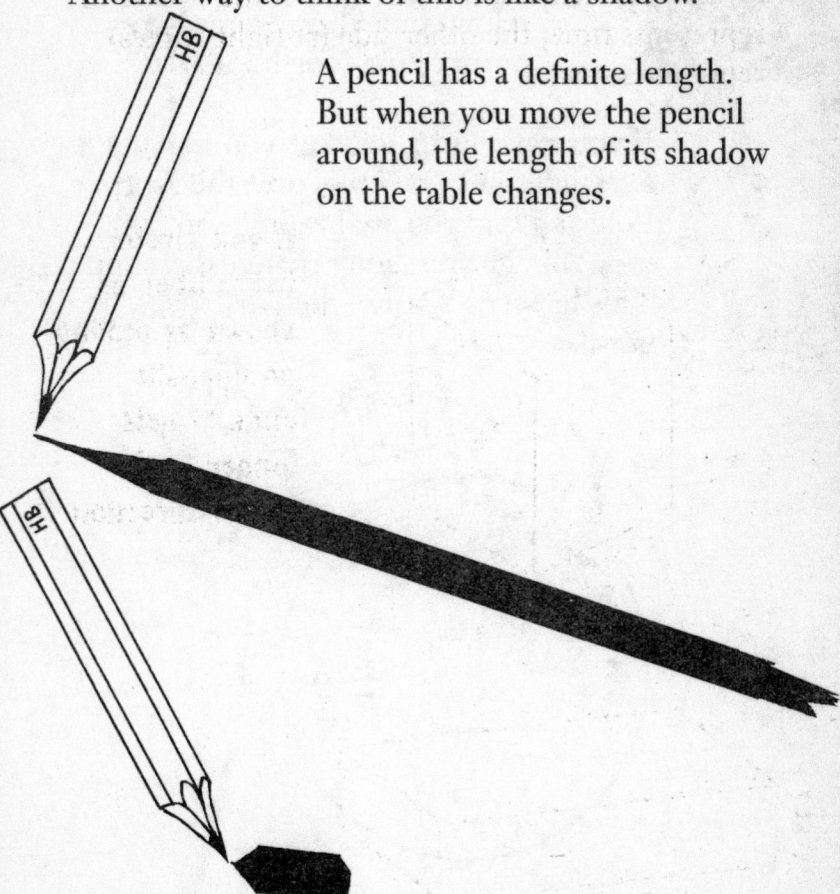

A pencil has a definite length. But when you move the pencil around, the length of its shadow on the table changes.

Everything has a four-dimensional length, called extension, which stays the same. When something moves, only the lengths of the shadows it makes in space and time change.

But I still don't understand why there was no time before the big bang.

Try an easier question first:

'How come there is nowhere north of the North Pole?'

If you walk north, and keep on walking in a straight line, you cross over the North Pole and find you are heading south - even though you didn't change direction! This happens because the Earth is not flat.

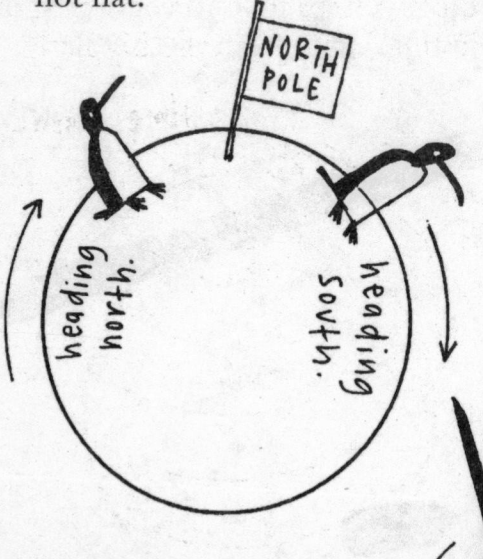

NORTH POLE

heading north.

heading south.

really?

The surface of the Earth is bent to make a sphere.

Many astronomers think that time is like that.
Spacetime is curved, like the surface of a sphere.

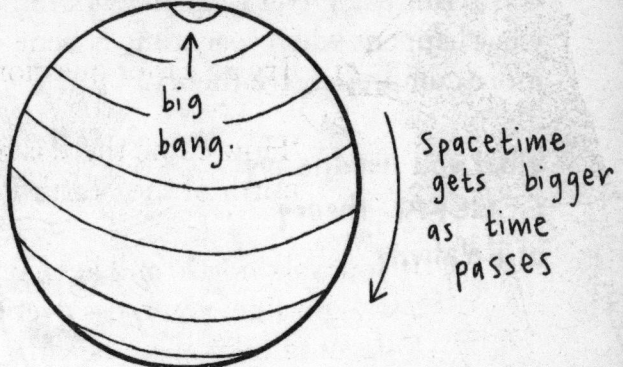

If you travelled back in time to the Big Bang, then
kept on going, you would find you were going
forwards in time, away from the Big Bang.

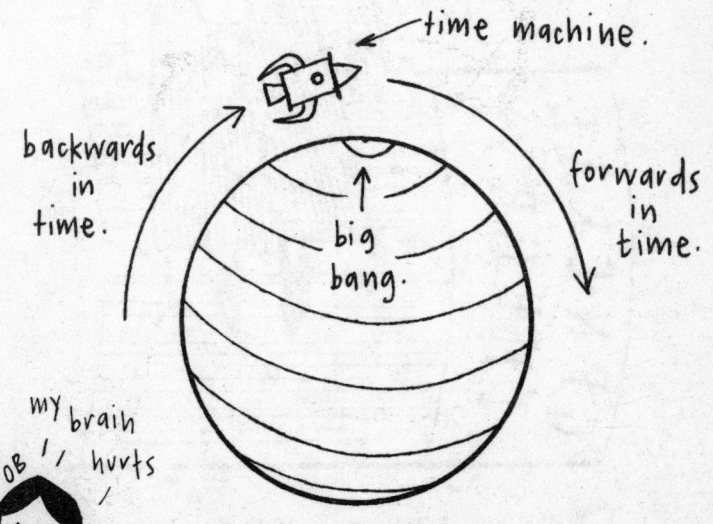

That is why there is no time before the
Big Bang, just as there is nowhere
north of the North Pole.

Einstein's Special Theory of Relativity describes how time stretches when space shrinks, and vice versa. But when you want to work out accurately what happens when spacetime is bent, you need a more comprehensive theory.

What you need is my GENERAL Theory of Relativity

Einstein's **General Theory of Relativity** explains everything included in the Special Theory, and more besides. It explains how **gravity** operates, and how the whole Universe works.

Imagine a stretched rubber sheet, like a trampoline.

Now put a heavy weight, like a bowling ball, on the sheet. It bends.

The gravity of a star like the Sun makes a similar dent in Spacetime.

If you tried to roll a marble across the rubber trampoline with the weight on it, the marble's track would be bent sideways by the dent in the rubber.

If a planet (or anything) moves past the Sun (or anything), the planet's track is bent sideways by the dent in spacetime. That's gravity.

The General Theory of Relativity is not just a wild idea. It has been tested in many experiments.

The most famous test happened in 1919 during an eclipse of the Sun. While the sky was dark, astronomers photographed the stars behind the Sun.

We found that the positions of the stars seemed to have been shifted slightly, compared with photographs of the same part of the sky when the Sun was not in the way.

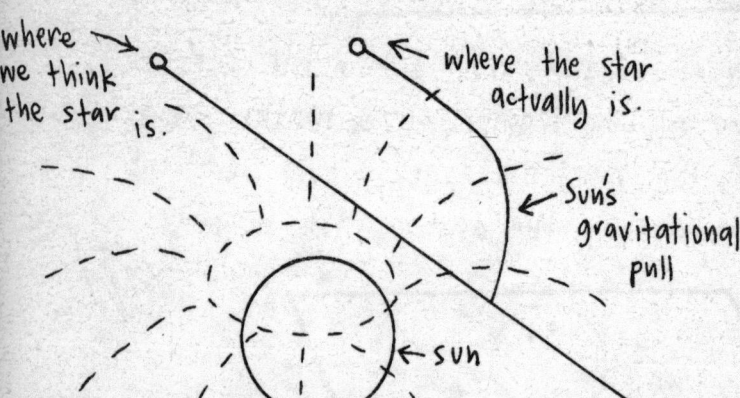

where we think the star is.

where the star actually is.

Sun's gravitational pull

← sun

The sideways shift was caused by the dent in spacetime made by the Sun. It happened because of the action of the Sun's gravity. The size of the shift exactly matched the prediction made by Einstein's theory.

The most accurate test of the General Theory was made in the 1980s.

Einstein's theory says that two very heavy stars orbiting one another very closely should make ripples in spacetime, called gravitational waves.

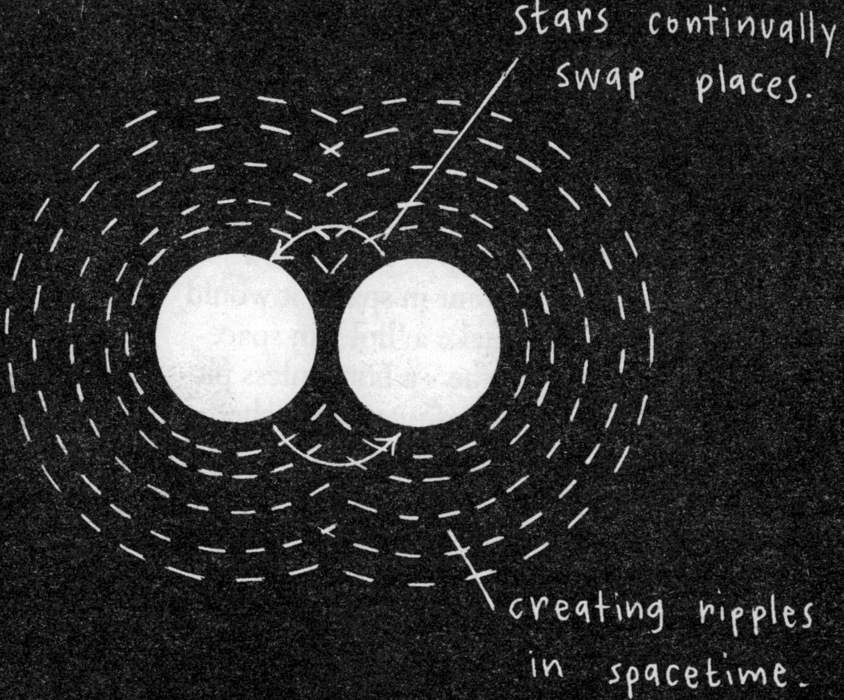

stars continually swap places.

creating ripples in spacetime.

Astronomers eventually found a double star just like this. It is called the binary pulsar. Careful measurements showed that it is making gravitational waves at exactly the rate predicted by Einstein's theory.

amazing!

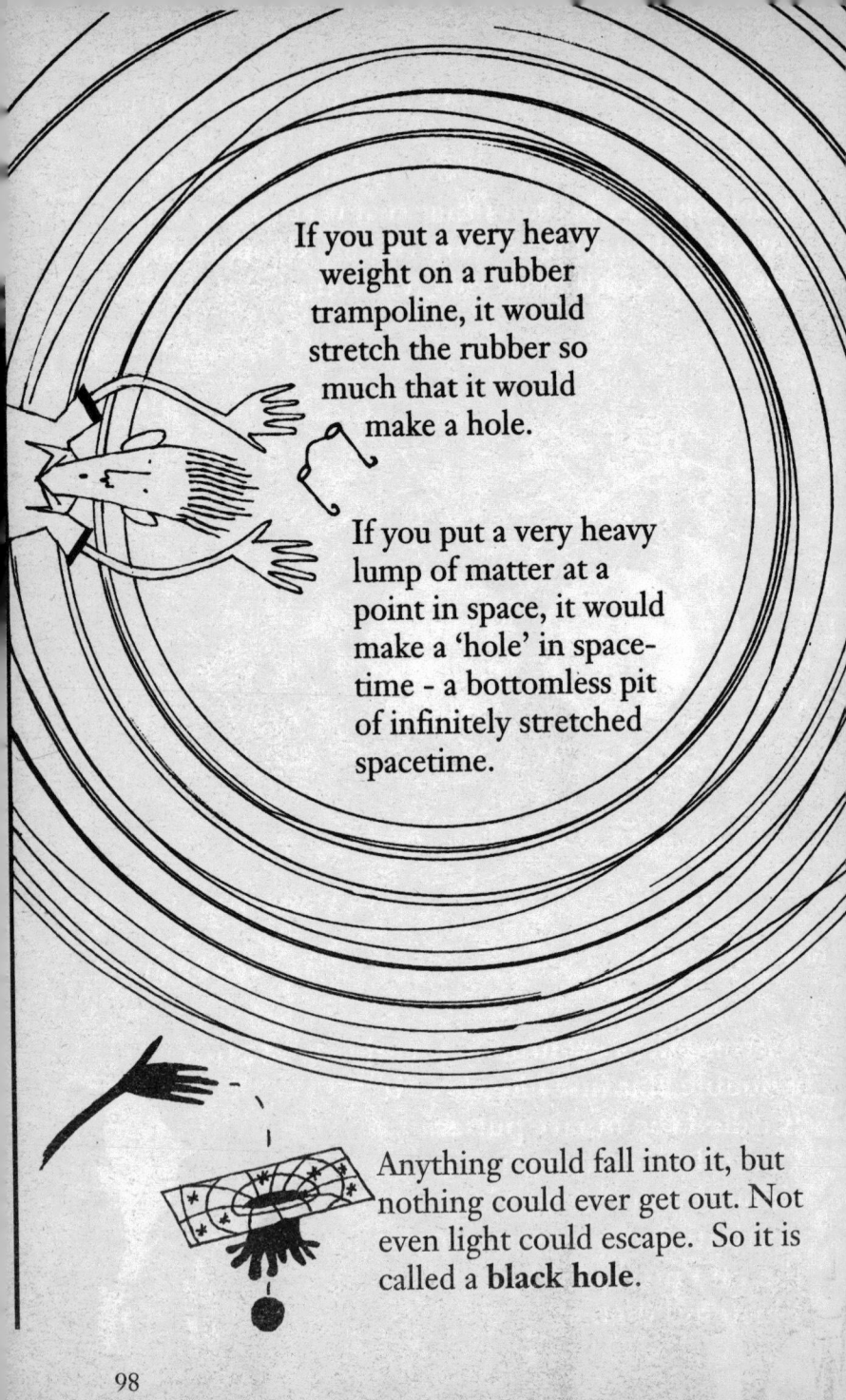

If you put a very heavy weight on a rubber trampoline, it would stretch the rubber so much that it would make a hole.

If you put a very heavy lump of matter at a point in space, it would make a 'hole' in space-time - a bottomless pit of infinitely stretched spacetime.

Anything could fall into it, but nothing could ever get out. Not even light could escape. So it is called a **black hole**.

You don't need very much matter to make a black hole. When a star has used up all its nuclear fuel, it cools down and shrinks into a small ball. If the ball of dead star stuff has as much matter in it as three stars like our Sun put together, it will make a black hole.

bright star.   cools down   and shrinks into a ball.

There are lots of stars around that are at least 10 times more massive than our Sun. Even if they blow some of their matter away into space to make new stars, some of them must still turn into black holes when they die.

Black holes really exist.

How can you prove they exist, when you can't see them?

tap
tap

Think of the tides. Sea tides on Earth are triggered by the movement of the Moon. As the Moon's phases change, the tides alter.

If the sky was always covered by cloud, you would never see the Moon. But the tides would still rise and fall in their regular rhythm. The tides are proof that the Moon exists, even if you can't see it.

A. LOW TIDE

whoa!

B. HIGH TIDE

HELP!

Some stars viewed through a large telescope seem to wobble as they move across the sky. Often, astronomers can see another star in orbit around the first one, tugging it to and fro.

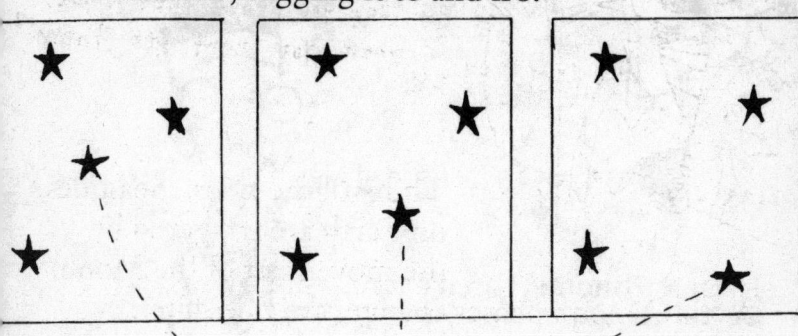

— Star Wobbles —

Sometimes the companion star can't be seen, but astronomers can still work out how much mass it contains from the way the first star wobbles. Often, it turns out that the invisible companion is a faint star about the same size as our Sun, too dim to be seen. But sometimes the invisible companion star is much bigger than our Sun. A star with that much mass would shine brightly enough to be seen.

So it must be a black hole!

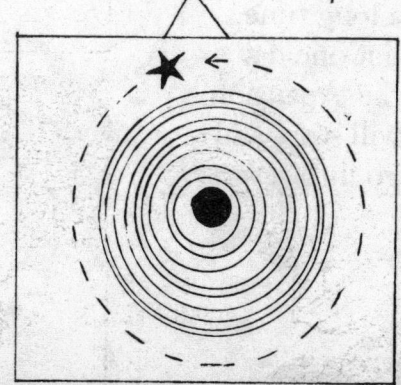

COR-

The future of time

How will the universe end?

the end is nigh.

I dunno. Sorry.

Even astronomers aren't sure.

Perhaps it will expand forever.
The galaxies will get further and
further apart, all the stars will die, and there will
be nothing left but blackness, the cold embers of
stars and planets, and black holes. Entropy will
have triumphed.

But if there is enough matter in the Universe, its
own gravity will bend spacetime around so that it
is closed. It would be like the inside of a black
hole. In that case, the Universe will
expand for
a long time,
but one day
the expansion
will stop, and
go into reverse.

INTO REVERSE?

ZOOM

1. Think of a tiny circle drawn around the North pole. This represents the size of the universe just after the big bang.

2. Further away from the pole the circles are bigger. This corresponds to the Universe expanding as time passes.

3. The circles are biggest around the equator.

4. But then as you go south (into the future) the circles shrink again.

5. At the south pole they vanish.

If time is like that, there is no time beyond the end of the Universe. Space and time will one day be swallowed up in a

BIG CRUNCH!

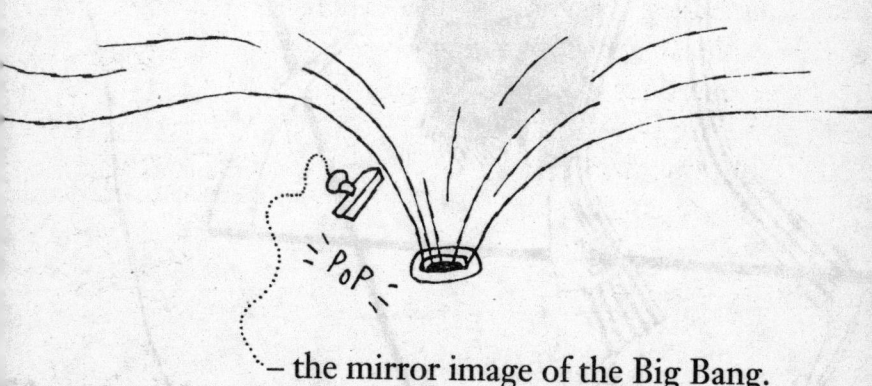

– the mirror image of the Big Bang.

BIG CRUNC

But the Big Crunch may not be the end of time.

If you tried to keep going south past the South Pole, you would find you were heading north again. In the same way, it's possible that the Universe might collapse 'through' the Big Crunch and find it was expanding outwards in a new Big Bang, with all the cosmic clocks re-set to zero.

Perhaps the Universe has 'bounced' like this many times already. 'Our' Big Bang may be just the latest in an endless cycle.

BIG BANG

POP

Our Universe may be a self-contained bubble of spacetime, like the skin of a soap bubble.

Black holes are also almost self-contained bubbles of spacetime, but they are connected to our Universe by the hole itself - a kind of throat, which swallows anything that comes near the hole.

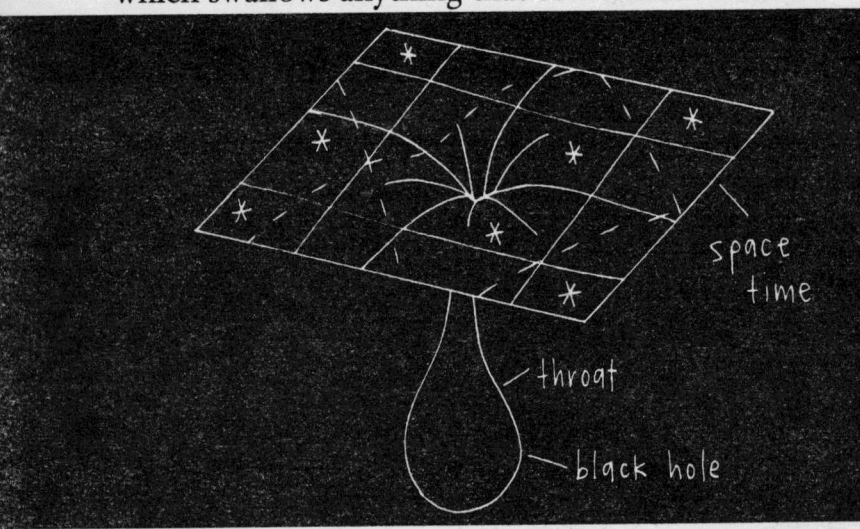

space time

throat

black hole

Anything that falls into a black hole is crushed by gravity. It is squeezed into a mathematical point, with no volume at all, at the centre of the hole. According to the General Theory of Relativity, stuff falling into a black hole could go right through it and be turned into the beginning of a completely new universe, in a new Big Bang.

This wouldn't mean that the stuff crushed into a black hole bounces back out into our Universe. It would be a different universe - another bubble of spacetime, connected to us by a tiny tunnel, called a **wormhole**.

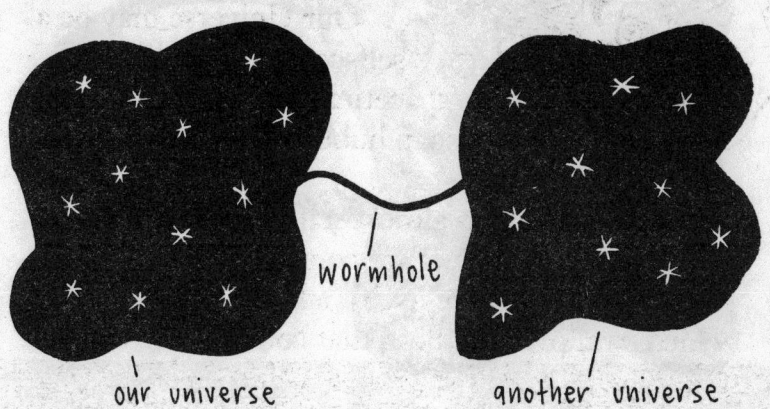

wormhole

our universe

another universe

If this happens every time a black hole forms, our Universe may be just one bubble in a froth of universes, like bubbles on a glass of beer, or frogspawn. Our Universe might even have been born out of a black hole in another universe.

wormholes

universes

Where does the other end of a black hole go to?
Some scientists think that black holes are the
gateways to tunnels to other universes.

wormhole
joins two
parts of our
universe

But why couldn't the tunnel come out in another
part of our own Universe? If wormholes like this
existed, it would be possible to jump in one end,
and come out of the other end, far away, near a
distant star.

It would take hardly any time at all to cross through the wormhole. It would be like a shortcut through space, a kind of cosmic subway.

Scientists didn't believe this was possible. But science fiction writers loved the idea. In the 1980s, the scientists decided to settle the question once and for all. They worked out all the equations that describe wormholes, using Einstein's General Theory of Relativity. They were embarrassed to discover that the equations do not forbid wormholes to exist. Tunnels through space really are allowed by the laws of physics.

The laws of physics say that black holes really could be the entrances to cosmic subways. But space is only one part of spacetime.

A hole through space is really a hole through spacetime. That means the other end of a wormhole could come out at a different time, not just a different place.

Or it could come out in the same place, but at a different time.

There is nothing in the laws of physics to make this impossible. This was such an amazing discovery that even the scientists who worked out the wormhole equations did not realise what it meant at first.

It means that there is nothing in the laws of physics which says that time travel is impossible. If you jumped into one end of a wormhole, you could come out of the other end not just any*where* in the Universe, but any*when* in the Universe.

There is another reason to get excited about wormholes. If you look out in one direction in space with a big telescope, you see galaxies billions of light years away.

If you look in the opposite direction, you see other galaxies billions of light years away. Studies of the light from galaxies show that the laws of physics are exactly the same on opposite sides of the Universe.

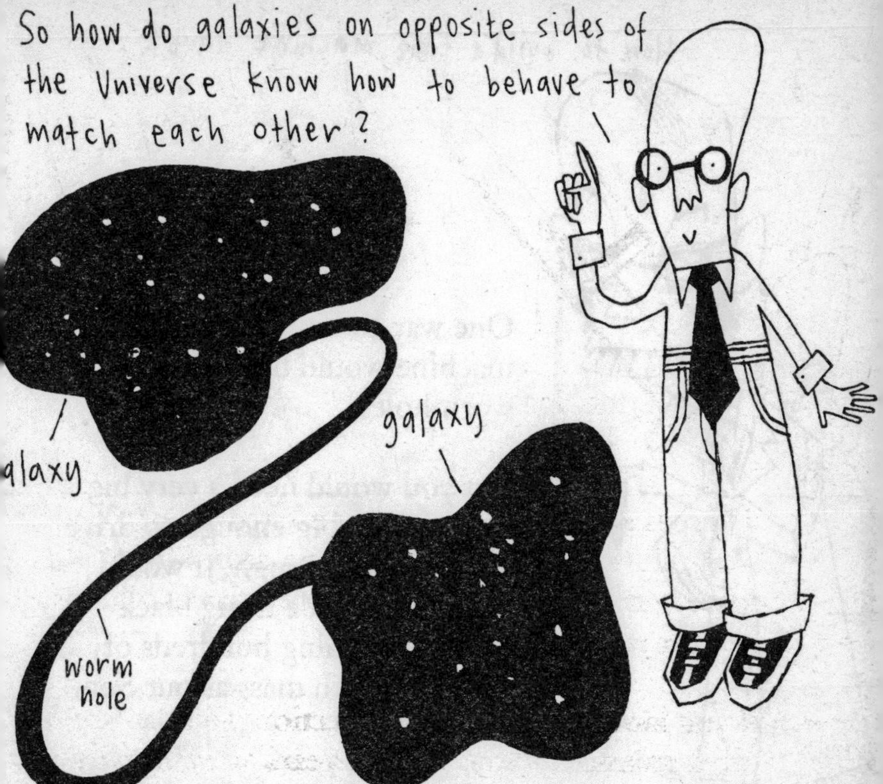

So how do galaxies on opposite sides of the Universe know how to behave to match each other?

galaxy

galaxy

worm hole

Perhaps the Universe is criss-crossed by tiny wormholes, too small even for an atom to get through, like a kind of cosmic spaghetti. News about what the laws of physics are could travel through all the worm holes, so that all the stars in all the galaxies, everywhere and everywhen, act the same.

Can we get back to time travel?

One way to build a time machine would be using wormholes.

But you would need a very big wormhole - big enough to drive a spaceship through. It would have to be made using black holes containing hundreds of times as much mass as our Sun.

There isn't much chance of actually making a wormhole this way. As well as needing a spaceship, you would need to be able to move whole stars around. If you could do that, you might as well look for a natural black hole, and tow it to where you want it. Then you would have to go to the other end of the wormhole, by diving through it in your spaceship, and then tow that end back home.

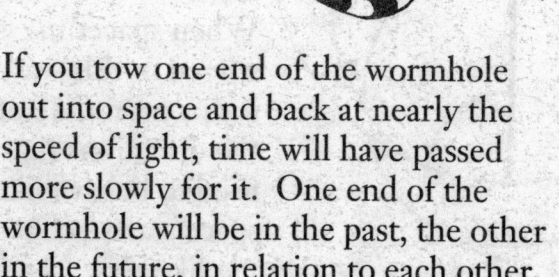

If you tow one end of the wormhole out into space and back at nearly the speed of light, time will have passed more slowly for it. One end of the wormhole will be in the past, the other in the future, in relation to each other.

You can travel in time, by going round and round the wormhole.

Here's another way to build a time machine.

If you had a long cylinder made of very dense stuff, and made it spin very fast, it would drag spacetime round in a kind of whirlpool (a bit like the way you can drag golden syrup round in a tin by stirring it).

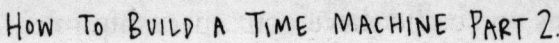

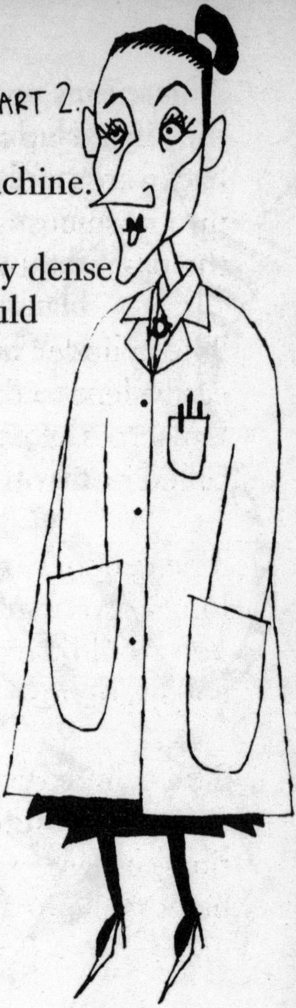

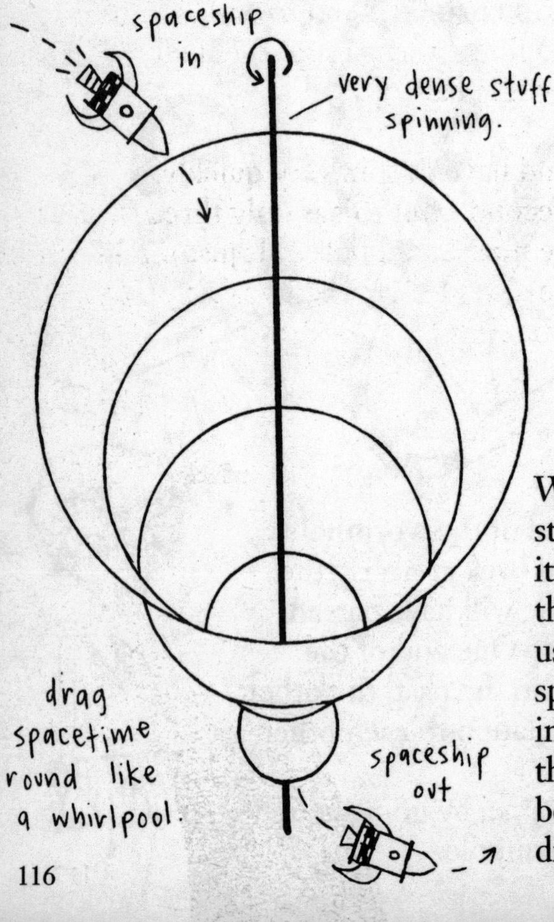

spaceship in

very dense stuff spinning.

drag spacetime round like a whirlpool.

spaceship out

When spacetime is stirred in this way, it tips over. One of the directions that used to behave like space starts behaving like time. And the time direction behaves like a space direction.

This means you could drive your spaceship into the stirred-up region near the cylinder, and drive backwards and forwards in time, then come out into normal spacetime at any time you wanted, in the past or future.

The cylinder would have to be very dense, equivalent to the whole Sun packed into a ball 10 km across. But such dense balls do exist - they are called **neutron stars**.

The cylinder would have to be at least 100 km long - ten neutron stars linked end to end. You would have to find a way to stop them all collapsing into a single ball.

The cylinder would have to spin very quickly, twice every millisecond. But this is only three times as fast as the most rapid pulsar. It just might be possible to take a fast pulsar and tweak it up to make a time machine!

er...

Yahoo! Well, what are we waiting for?

But time travel would cause paradoxes.

Paradox:
A seemingly absurd or contradictory statement, even if actually well founded.

Suppose you travelled back in time, and your time machine landed on top of your granny when she was a little girl.

COO

IF YOUR GRANNY DIED WHEN SHE WAS A GIRL, YOUR MOTHER WOULD NEVER HAVE BEEN BORN.

I come in peace

what do you mean? You killed Agnes

SO YOU WOULD NEVER HAVE BEEN BORN.

! hey!

POP

SO YOU WOULDN'T GO BACK IN TIME AND YOUR GRANNY WOULDN'T BE KILLED.

YAHOO

Some scientists think that because of paradoxes there must be a law of physics that forbids time travel. Others think that there could just be a law that prevents paradoxes so you couldn't kill your own granny.

We won't be sure who is right until someone succeeds in building a time machine!

SO YOU WOULD BE BORN!

Today we understand Time and the Universe better than at any time in the past. But there is still much more to be found out. Some mysteries will be left for future generations to solve - but who knows what amazing discoveries will be made in your lifetime?

HELLO. I am you, 60 years in the future. I've come back to tell you to pay attention in Physics because you'll discover time travel later on.

~ holey moley.

Key dates in the History of Time

3000 BC First stage of Stonehenge built

500 BC Pythagorians say that the Earth is a sphere

235 BC Eratosthenes calculates the size of
the Earth

46 BC Julian calendar introduced

1066 Comet now known as Halley's Comet seen

1473 Nicolaus Copernicus born

1581 Galileo studies the swing of a pendulum

1582 Gregorian calendar introduced in most
of Europe

1642 Isaac Newton born

1650s Christiaan Huygens invents an accurate
pendulum clock

1656 Edmond Halley born

1676 First measurement of the speed of light

1735 John Harrison builds his first chronometer

1752 Gregorian calendar introduced in Britain

1783 John Michell is the first person to predict
what are now known as black holes

1820 Royal Astronomical Society founded mid-19th
century Thermodynamics and Entropy studied

1864 James Clerk Maxwell discovers the equations
that describe how electromagnetic radiation,
including light, moves through space

1879 Albert Einstein born

1884 Greenwich Meridian established as the "prime meridian"

1905 Special Theory of Relativity

1907 Hermann Minkowski realises that time is the fourth dimension

1915 General Theory of Relativity

1916 Discovery that the general theory predicts what are now known as black holes

1919 Bending of starlight observed during a solar eclipse

1929 Discovery that the Universe is expanding

1940s Theory of the Big Bang developed and named

1958 NASA founded

1967 Pulsars discovered

1967 The second is defined in terms of an atomic clock

1967 Black holes named by John Wheeler, even though not yet discovered

1971 First identification of a black hole — the invisible companion to a star known as HDE 226868

1974 American Frank Tipler suggests the possibility of a rotating cylinder time machine

1988 Scientists at Caltech suggest the possibility of a wormhole time machine

1992 Big Bang theory confirmed by observations made by NASA's COBE satellite

Glossary

Big Bang   The beginning of the Universe, when everything (including space and time and matter) burst out from a point.

Big Crunch   The end of the Universe, when everything will collapse into a point. Don't worry, it won't happen for at least 100 billion years.

Billion   One thousand million. 1,000,000,000.

Black hole   An object where gravity is so strong that nothing can escape, not even light.

Chronometer   A very accurate watch.

Circadian rhythm   Literally, a rhythm that takes about a day. The best example is our pattern of waking and sleeping.

DNA   Short for deoxyribonucleic acid. The name of the molecule in every cell of your body which carries the information which tells your body how to work.

Entropy   The amount of untidiness in the Universe. Entropy always increases.

Galaxy   A huge group of stars in outer space. There are hundreds of thousands of millions of galaxies in the Universe and each galaxy contains millions of stars. The Sun is just one ordinary star in the Milky Way galaxy.

Gravity   The force that pulls us down on Earth and gives us weight. It also holds the Earth and other planets in orbit around the Sun in the Solar System.

Gravitational waves   Ripples in space made by very heavy objects, like pulsars, in orbit around one another.

Greenwich Mean Time (GMT)   The time by the Sun at the meridian which runs through the old Royal Observatory at Greenwich in England. It is noon GMT when the Sun is highest in the sky over Greenwich.

Hemisphere   Half a sphere. On Earth, the Northern

Hemisphere is everything north of the equator, and the Southern Hemisphere is everything south of the equator.

International Date Line A line roughly following the meridian on the other side of the world from Greenwich, at 180 degrees of longitude. If you cross the line going east, the date goes back a day; if you cross the line going west, the date goes forward a day.

Latitude How far north or south of the equator a place is. A line of latitude is any imaginary line running right around the world from west to east, parallel to the equator.

Light year The distance light can travel in one year. About 9.46 thousand billion kilometres. The nearest star (apart from the Sun) is more than 4 light years away.

Longitude How far east or west of Greenwich a place is. A line of longitude is any imaginary line running right around the world over the poles, at right angles to the equator.

Meridian Half of a line of longitude, from the North Pole to the South Pole.

Neutron star A tiny star left over after the explosion of a supernova. A neutron star is only about 10 km across, but it has as much matter in it as our Sun. Pulsars are neutron stars.

Orbit The path followed by a planet going round a star, or by a moon going round a planet. These orbits are elliptical.

Planet A cool body in space that orbits around a star.

Pulsar A small, very heavy star (about 10 km across) which spins very quickly and flicks round abeam of radio waves, like a cosmic lighthouse.

Red Giant An old star which has swollen up to a huge size. The Sun will become a Red Giant in about 5 billion years from now, and will burn up the Earth.

Red Shift A change in the spectrum of light from an object, which moves the patterns in the spectrum towards the red end of the rainbow and away from the blue end.

REM sleep A kind of sleep that occurs when you are dreaming, and which causes Rapid Eye Movement.

Second Law of Thermodynamics Scientific version of the rule that things wear out.

Solar System The Sun and everything that is in orbit around the Sun, including the Earth and eight other planets.

Spacetime A combination of space and time used in the theory of relativity. Albert Einstein showed that time is like the fourth dimension.

Spectrum The pattern made when light is spread out into a rainbow by passing it through a triangular wedge of glass or plastic (a prism).

Star A hot object in space that shines because it is hot. The Sun is a star.

Sun The nearest star, which the Earth orbits. The Sun is an ordinary star. It only looks so bright because it is much closer to us than other stars. The Sun is about 100 times bigger across than the Earth is.

Supernova The explosion of a very large star.

Theory of Relativity The science that describes how space and time work.

Time zone A region where all the clocks are set to the same time for convenience. All of Britain, for example, is in the same time zone, even though the Sun rises earlier in the eastern part of the country and later in the west.

Universe Everything there is in space. All the stars and all the planets and all the galaxies.

White Dwarf A very old star, after it has been a Red Giant, that has run out of fuel and shrunk down into a ball no bigger than the Earth.

Wormhole A tunnel through spacetime.

Finding out more

Non Fiction:

Kate Charlesworth & John Gribbin, The Cartoon History of Time (Macdonald, London, 1990)

John & Mary Gribbin, Time & Space (Dorling Kindersley, London, 1994)

Robin Kerrod, The Big Book of Stars and Planets (Hamlyn, London, 1990)

Patrick Moore, The Guinness Book of Astronomy (Guinness, London, 1992)

James Muirden, Our Universe (Ward Lock, London, 1978)

Dava Sobel, Longitude (Bloomsbury, London, 1996)

James Trefil, 1001 Things Everyone Should Know About Science (Cassell, London, 1993)

Science Fiction:

Gregory Benford, Timescape (Penguin, London, 1980).

H. G. Wells, The Time Machine (various editions)

INDEX

time to go home

WOOF WOOF